W9-BNR-471

THE **FONDUE** COOKBOOK

THE **FONDUE** COOKBOOK

BY GINA STEER

CONTEMPORARY BOOKS

Library of Congress Cataloging-in-Publication Data

Steer, Gina

    The fondue cookbook : over 100 no-fuss fondue recipes for fun entertaining / by Gina Steer.

      p. cm.

ISBN 0-8092-2442-9

Reprinted 2002

1. Fondue. I. Title.

TX825 S78 1999

641.8'1—dc21

99-059932

A QUINTET BOOK

This book was designed and produced by
Quintet Publishing Limited
6 Blundell Street
London N7 9BH

Creative Director: Richard Dewing
Art Director: Paula Marchant
Designer: Deep Design
Project Editor: Amanda Dixon
Editor: Margaret Gilbey
Photographer: Ian Garlick
Food Stylist: Kathryn Hawkins

Typeset in Great Britain by Central Southern Typesetters, Eastbourne
Manufactured in Singapore by Regent Publishing Services Ltd.
Printed in China by Leefung-Asco Printers Trading Ltd.

Published by Contemporary Books
A division of NTC/Contemporary Publishing Group, Inc.
4255 West Touhy Avenue, Lincolnwood (Chicago), Illinois 60712-1975
U.S.A.
Copyright © 1999 by Quintet Publishing Limited

All rights reserved. No part of this book may be reproduced, stored in a retrieval system, or transmitted in any form or by any means, electronic, mechanical, photocopying, recording, or otherwise, without the prior written permission of NTC/Contemporary Publishing Group, Inc.

Printed in China by Leefung-Asco Printers Trading Limited
International Standard Book Number: 0-8092-2442-9

01 02 03   19 18 17 16 15 14 13 12 11 10 9 8 7 6

AUTHOR'S ACKNOWLEDGMENTS

With thanks to Le Creuset for providing help and information relating to the history and tradition of the fondue. Many thanks to my family and friends in the tasting of all the fondues.

Some recipes in this book use raw eggs. Because of the slight risk of salmonella, raw eggs should not be served to the very young, the ill or the elderly, or to pregnant women.

CONTENTS

INTRODUCTION

Fondues of all kinds are enjoyed throughout the world today. However, the dish originated many centuries ago in Switzerland as a result of the country's climate and geography, and fondue is now the Swiss national dish.

The harsh winters of the Alpine mountains meant small isolated villages could be cut off from the outside world for months at a time and food supplies were limited. The only readily available ingredients in many villages were cheese, wine, and bread. As the winter dragged on, the cheese made in the summer began to dry out. The villagers needed to find a dish that would be both filling and sustaining but which also tasted good—hence the birth of fondue. The word *fondue* comes from the French word *fondre*, meaning to melt or to blend. The original Swiss fondue came from the region of Neuchâtel and was made with Gruyère and Emmentaler cheese. Other villages soon adopted the dish and created their own versions, using local cheese and produce.

Nowadays, we can find many varieties of fondue, and in this book I have featured a selection of my favorites. France is famous for its Fondue Bourguignonne (page 30), in which strips of prime steak are cooked in hot oil, then dipped into a savory sauce. The Asian version (page 48) uses a Mongolian hot pot to cook the food in a fragrantly flavored broth; other fondues consist of vegetables and meat dipped into a Japanese-style tempura batter and cooked in sizzling oil. Then there are deliciously wicked chocolate and fruit fondues. As a matter of fact, almost any food can be cooked in a fondue pot, making it an easy and fun way to entertain your family and friends.

To keep a cheese fondue creamy, you must swirl the dippers in a figure of eight when dipping. Tradition has it that if you have the misfortune to lose your dipper in the fondue you have to pay a forfeit—a woman must kiss all the men present and a man must give the hostess either a bottle of wine or a glass of kirsch; if anyone loses their dipper again, they have to host the next fondue party.

While the fondue is sitting on the denatured alcohol burner, a delicious crust is formed on the base of the pot. This is considered to be the greatest delicacy of the entire meal and should be shared among all the guests.

It is traditional not to drink cold drinks while eating, as it was always believed they would cause indigestion. Instead, unsweetened tea, warm fruit juice, or even mulled wine would be served with the food, and a glass of cherry brandy, schnapps, or kirschwasser would be offered in a "rest period" halfway through the meal. However, a glass of the wine used in making the fondue would be an excellent accompaniment, preferably served at room temperature.

GUIDELINES

There are a variety of shapes and types of fondue pots available, even one designed especially for chocolate fondues. Whichever pot you have, there are a few guidelines to follow when using it.

- Before starting to use your fondue pot, read the manufacturer's instructions carefully and always take great care when transferring any hot oil or broth to the pot.
- Light the denatured alcohol burner carefully and place on the table on a heatproof mat or surface. Never add extra fuel to the burner while it is lit or still hot.
- Do not used a damaged burner and when moving the hot fondue pot, handle with oven gloves or a thick cloth.
- Cheese and chocolate fondues burn easily and should be kept warm over a low heat.

CHEESE FONDUES

- When making a cheese fondue, use a heavy-based pan, metal-lined, with an enamel or a cast-iron base, or a heavy-glazed earthenware pot, as this will prevent the cheese from burning.
- Use strong-flavored cheese: melt it slowly and once the fondue is transferred to the denatured alcohol burner ensure it bubbles *gently*. Do not let it boil, or the cheese will become stringy. If this does happen, lower the heat and continue to cook gently until the cheese has melted and the mixture becomes smooth.
- Always choose a dry wine or cider, and do not worry if at first the cheese separates from the wine: just keep stirring and it will gradually become smooth and creamy.
- If the cheese forms a lump in the base of the pot, increase the heat slightly and keep stirring. If it curdles, add a teaspoonful of lemon juice and beat well; this should rescue your fondue.

- If the fondue becomes too thick, add a little extra warmed wine or cider; if it is too thin, add a little extra cornstarch, blended with a small amount of water.
- Bread for dipping should not be too fresh or it will crumble in the fondue. Salads should be offered as an accompaniment. If you realize your guests are still hungry (though fondues *are* very filling!), serve a fruit dessert of your choice.
- Any left-over cheese fondue can be chilled and used in soups, as a filling for potatoes baked in their skins; or in tomato-based sauces.
- Remember all fondues are very hot, so take care not to burn the mouth.

MEAT, FISH, & SEAFOOD FONDUES

- Fondues such as Mongolian Chicken Hot Pot that are cooked in simmering broth require pots that transmit heat quickly and keep the cooking liquid at its highest temperature. The pots should be filled to just over half full. Take care not to overfill.
- When using oil, the temperature should be around 350 to 375°F. If no thermometer is available, drop a small cube of bread into the oil. The bread will turn golden in about 30 seconds if the oil is at the correct temperature.
- Unless otherwise specified, use a vegetable oil of your choice.
- If liked, a little flavored oil can be added to the basic cooking oil.
- For meat or fish, choose good-quality meat that cooks quickly and firm fish that will not disintegrate during cooking. These fondues are much enhanced when served with dips and sauces in which the cooked food can be rolled before eating.
- To prevent the food spitting, meat and fish should be dried before cooking in the hot oil. If too much food is put into the hot oil at any one time, it will lower the temperature and you may find the oil will need reheating on the stove.

DESSERT FONDUES

- If you do not have a specific chocolate fondue pot (these have a maximum chocolate fill level and are a slightly different shape from regular pots), then any fondue pot will work well for desserts.
- As a general rule, do not boil dessert fondues as this will impair the flavor; they are designed to be eaten warm, not hot. Remember chocolate burns very easily.
- If you chill fresh fruit dippers before serving, you will find the chocolate will coat the fruit more easily.

Eating fondue should be fun—so browse through the recipes in this book and pick out a few tempting ideas to try, invite some friends over, and enjoy a great, fun-packed, delicious informal party.

FISH &
SEAFOOD

THAI JUMBO SHRIMP FONDUE

THIS IS A FONDUE WITH A DIFFERENCE—HERE THE SHRIMP ARE COOKED IN A BROTH, THEN BEAN SPROUTS AND NOODLES ARE ADDED AT THE END OF COOKING.

Devein the shrimp, rinse lightly, and pat dry with paper towels. Place in small bowls, garnish with lime wedges and sprigs of fresh cilantro, cover, and leave in the refrigerator.

Place the gingerroot, lemon grass, chiles, garlic, lime zest, and broth in a Mongolian hot pot and bring to a boil. Simmer for 15 minutes then stir in the chopped cilantro. Place over the lit burner.

Combine all the ingredients for the dipping sauce and set aside.

Cook the noodles in boiling water for 3 minutes or until cooked, drain, and place aside.

Spear the shrimp onto the forks and cook for 1 to 2 minutes in the hot broth then dip into the dipping sauce before eating.

When all the shrimp have been cooked, add the noodles and bean sprouts to the pot, heat for 1 to 2 minutes, then ladle into soup bowls and serve as soup.

Serves **6**
Preparation time **5 minutes**
Cooking time **20 to 22 minutes**

2 lbs raw jumbo shrimp, peeled
1 Tbsp grated gingerroot
2 stalks lemon grass
1 to 3 Thai chiles, seeded and chopped
2 to 3 garlic cloves, peeled
Grated zest of $\frac{1}{2}$ lime
3 cups fish broth or water
3 Tbsp chopped fresh cilantro
1 cup dried thread egg noodles
1 cup bean sprouts

DIPPING SAUCE
1 Tbsp soy sauce
2 tsp fish sauce or $\frac{1}{2}$ tsp salt
2 tsp liquid honey, warmed
1 Thai chile, seeded and chopped

TO GARNISH
Lime wedges and sprigs of fresh cilantro

CRISPY SCAMPI FONDUE

SCAMPI CAN BE QUITE DIFFICULT TO SKEWER ONTO THE FONDUE FORK: TRY SKEWERING THREE TO FOUR AT A TIME BEFORE COOKING.

Devein the shrimp, rinse lightly, dry thoroughly on paper towels, and reserve. Mix together the lemon zest, chiles, flour, and seasoning. Roll the shrimp in the flour mixture and leave for at least 30 minutes.

Place the beaten egg and the bread crumbs in two separate shallow dishes. Dip the shrimp in the beaten egg, allowing any excess egg to drip back into the bowl, then coat in the bread crumbs. Place in a serving bowl and garnish with parsley sprigs.

Heat the oil in the fondue pot then transfer the pot to the lit burner in order to keep it hot.

Each guest can now spear the shrimp with their forks and cook them in the hot oil for 1 to 2 minutes or until golden and crisp. Serve with the Tartar Sauce, lemon wedges, and pita bread filled with lettuce, cucumber, and cherry tomatoes.

Serves **4 as a main course or 8 as an appetizer**
Preparation time **10 minutes plus 30 minutes marinating time**
Cooking time **2 to 3 minutes per piece**

1 lb raw jumbo shrimp, peeled
2 Tbsp lemon zest
1½ tsp dried crushed chiles
2 Tbsp white all-purpose flour
Salt and freshly ground black pepper
2 medium eggs, beaten
½ cup dried bread crumbs
1 pt oil, for frying

TO GARNISH
Parsley sprigs.

TO SERVE
Tartar Sauce *(see page 100)*, **lemon wedges, warm pita bread filled with shredded lettuce, cucumber strips, and quartered cherry tomatoes.**

DRUNKEN HADDOCK FONDUE

LOOK FOR THICK FILLETS OF FISH FOR THIS FONDUE AND CUT INTO THICK CUBES.

Serves **4 to 6**
Preparation time **35 minutes**
Cooking time **2 to 3 minutes**
  per piece

1½ lb smoked haddock fillets,
  skinned and bones discarded
  (reserve the trimmings)
1 large carrot
1 medium onion
1 small bunch fresh herbs
A few black peppercorns
1 cup dry white wine
2 cups water

TO GARNISH
Lemon wedges and fresh
  chervil sprigs.

TO SERVE
Creamy Herb Mayonnaise
  (see page 104), **warm crusty**
  bread, and assorted salads.

Rinse the fish and pat dry. Cut into large cubes or strips. Place the fish in small bowls, garnish with lemon wedges and chervil, cover, and refrigerate until required.

Peel and slice the carrot and onion, and place in a large pan with the fish trimmings, herbs, peppercorns, wine, and water. Bring to a boil and simmer for at least 30 minutes. Strain into the fondue pot and place on the lit burner.

Spear the fish onto the fondue forks and cook in the hot broth for 2 to 3 minutes. Serve with the mayonnaise, bread, and salads.

ASIAN FISH HOT POT FONDUE

USE AN ASSORTMENT OF FISH THAT PROVIDE A GOOD VARIETY OF COLORS AND TEXTURES.

Serves **6**
Preparation time **15 minutes**
Cooking time **22 to 23 minutes**

2 lbs assorted fish fillet such
  as cod, salmon, angler fish,
  and scallops
1 large carrot, peeled and sliced
1 large onion, peeled and sliced
2 Thai chiles, seeded and sliced
A few fresh parsley sprigs
4 star anise
1 tsp whole peppercorns
1 Tbsp grated gingerroot

3 cups water
4 Tbsp dry sherry
1 Tbsp soy sauce

TO GARNISH
Fresh cilantro sprigs and
  lime wedges.

TO SERVE
Glutinous (short-grain) rice and
  Mixed Chinese Green Salad
  (see page 108).

Skin the fish, reserving the trimmings, and discard any bones. Clean scallops if using. Cut the fish into cubes, place in small bowls, and garnish with cilantro sprigs and lime wedges. Cover and refrigerate until required.

Place the carrot, onion and chiles in the Mongolian hot pot with the fish trimmings, the parsley, remaining spices, and the water. Bring to a boil, then simmer for 20 minutes or until the broth has reduced by about one third. Strain and return to the pot, then stir in the sherry and soy sauce.

Heat the broth, then place over the lit burner, and gently simmer.

Spear the fish onto the fondue forks, cook in the broth for 2 to 3 minutes. Serve with the rice and salad.

SALMON LAKSA FONDUE

THIS FONDUE PROVIDES AN INTERESTING AND FUN MEAL THAT BOTH FRIENDS AND FAMILY WILL LOVE. THE AROMATIC FLAVORS OF THE ASIAN SPICES GENTLY PERFUME THE SALMON AS IT COOKS IN THE COCONUT MILK.

Place the coconut milk with the chiles, gingerroot, lemon grass, star anise, shallots, and carrot in a pan and simmer gently for 15 minutes. Remove from the heat and allow to infuse for 15 minutes, then strain into the fondue pot.

Place the fondue pot over the lit burner and allow to heat through. Discard any bones from the salmon, rinse lightly, and pat dry on paper towels. Cut into cubes.

Mix the cilantro and cornstarch together then use to coat the salmon. Leave to marinate for 45 minutes.

Spear the salmon onto fondue forks or wooden skewers and cook in the flavored coconut mix for 2 to 3 minutes. Serve with the Mixed Chinese Green Salad.

Serves **4 to 6**
Preparation time **6 to 8 minutes plus 15 minutes infusing time and 45 minutes marinating time**
Cooking time **2 to 3 minutes per piece**

1 pt unsweetened coconut milk
2 Thai chiles, seeded and chopped
1 Tbsp grated gingerroot
2 stalks lemon grass, chopped
3 to 4 star anise
3 to 4 shallots, peeled and chopped
1 large carrot, grated
1 lb 4 oz fresh salmon fillet, skinned
2 Tbsp chopped fresh cilantro
2 Tbsp cornstarch

TO SERVE
Mixed Chinese Green Salad *(see page 108).*

BOSTON CHOWDER FONDUE

AN IDEAL SUPPER TO SERVE WHEN YOU WISH TO HAVE AN INFORMAL GATHERING—FRESH OR CANNED CLAMS
WORK WELL IN THIS FONDUE. IF USING FRESH CLAMS, PREPARE AND COOK THEM BEFORE USING.

Serves **6**
Preparation time **5 minutes**
Cooking time **8 to 10 minutes**

½ stick butter
8 scallions, trimmed and chopped
6 Tbsp white all-purpose flour
1½ cups milk
1¼ lbs canned or live clams,
   freshly cooked
½ cup clam liquor (if using canned clams)
3 Tbsp lemon juice
¾ cup corn kernels
2 Tbsp chopped fresh parsley
A few drops of Tabasco Sauce
Salt and freshly ground black pepper

TO SERVE
Cooked baby new potatoes, strips of red and
   green bell pepper, and celery sticks for dipping.

Place the butter in the fondue pot over a
gentle heat and cook, stirring until melted.
Add the scallions and cook for 2 minutes.
Stir in the flour and cook for 2 minutes.

Gradually stir in the milk, bring to a boil, and
simmer for 2 minutes. Drain the clams if using
canned, reserving the liquor, then stir the liquor
into the pot with the lemon juice, corn kernels,
parsley, Tabasco Sauce, and seasoning. Cook
for 2 to 3 minutes or until the corn is cooked.

Stir in the clams, place the pot over the lit
burner, and cook for a few minutes to heat
through. Serve with potatoes, bell pepper strips,
and celery sticks.

SOLE & ORANGE FONDUE

SOLE IS A DELICATE FISH AND ONLY REQUIRES THE MINIMUM
OF COOKING. LEAVE THE SKIN ON THE FISH AND CUT INTO
STRIPS SO IT CAN BE THREADED ONTO THE FONDUE FORKS
AND WILL NOT FALL OFF INTO THE POT DURING COOKING.

Serves **4**
Preparation time **8 to 10 minutes plus**
   30 minutes marinating time
Cooking time **1 to 2 minutes per piece**

1½ lbs sole fillets
Grated zest of 1 large orange
4 Tbsp orange juice
1 Tbsp liquid orange
   blossom honey, warmed
2 tsp cornstarch
Salt and freshly ground black pepper
1 pt sunflower oil, for frying

TO GARNISH
Orange wedges and tarragon sprigs.

TO SERVE
Freshly cooked baby new potatoes,
   Green Mayonnaise *(see page 96)*
   and Avocado & Mango Salad
   (see page 106).

Rinse the fish lightly and pat dry on paper towels. Cut into strips and
place aside.

Mix the orange zest, juice, honey, cornstarch, and seasoning together
and pour over the sole strips. Leave to marinate for 30 minutes. Place
in small bowls and garnish with orange wedges and tarragon sprigs.

Heat the oil in the fondue pot, then transfer to the lit burner.

Thread the sole strips onto the fondue forks and cook in the hot oil for 1 to
2 minutes, or until crisp. Serve with the potatoes, salad, and mayonnaise.

CRISPY SMOKED FISH FONDUE

THIS IS AN IDEAL FONDUE TO PREPARE AHEAD, LEAVING YOU PLENTY OF TIME TO ENJOY ENTERTAINING YOUR GUESTS.

Discard the skin from the fish and flake into small pieces. Set aside.

Melt the butter in a small pan, then stir in the flour and cook for 2 minutes. Take off the heat and gradually stir in the milk, then return to the heat and cook, stirring until thick and glossy.

Remove from the heat and stir in the reserved fish, the lemon zest, anchovy essence, scallions, and parsley. Mix lightly, then turn into a bowl, cover lightly, and refrigerate for at least 30 minutes, longer if time permits.

Place the egg and bread crumbs in two separate shallow bowls. Form the chilled fish mixture into small balls, then dip into the beaten egg, allowing any excess to drip back into the bowl, and then coat in the bread crumbs. Chill until required.

Heat the oil in the fondue pot, then place over the lit burner. Spear the fish balls onto skewers and cook in the hot oil for 2 to 3 minutes or until crisp. Garnish with the lemon wedges and serve with the Tartar Sauce, coleslaw, and French fries.

Serves **4 to 6**

Preparation time **15 minutes plus 30 minutes marinating time**

Cooking time **2 to 3 minutes per piece plus 5 minutes for sauce**

¾ **lb smoked mackerel fillet**

½ **stick butter**

½ **cup white flour**

1 cup milk

Grated zest of 1 lemon

1 tsp anchovy essence

6 scallions, chopped fine

1 Tbsp chopped fresh parsley

2 medium eggs, beaten

¾ **cup dried natural white bread crumbs**

1 pt oil, for frying

TO GARNISH

Lemon wedges.

TO SERVE

Tartar Sauce *(see page 100)*, **Zesty Orange Coleslaw** *(see page 114)*, **and French fries.**

MIXED FISH FONDUE

COATING THE FISH IN CORNSTARCH HELPS KEEP THE FISH TOGETHER WHILE COOKING.

Serves **6 to 8**
Preparation time **15 minutes**
   plus 15 minutes marinating time
Cooking time **2 to 4 minutes per piece**

2 lbs assorted fish such as angler
   fish, salmon, cod, jumbo shrimp,
   and scallops
2 large egg whites
2 to 3 tsp Tabasco Sauce, or to taste
2 to 3 Tbsp chopped fresh cilantro
3 Tbsp cornstarch
1 pt oil, for frying

TO GARNISH
Parsley sprigs and lemon
   wedges.

TO SERVE
Sour Cream Sauce *(see page*
   103), **Artichoke & Bean**
   Salad with Vinaigrette *(see*
   page 110), **and freshly**
   cooked rice.

Trim the fish, discarding any bones. Peel and devein the shrimp if using. Rinse lightly and dry on paper towels. Cut into cubes and place in a shallow dish.

Beat the egg whites, then stir in the Tabasco Sauce and cilantro. Place the cornstarch into a bowl, then beat in the egg white mixture.

Pour the egg white mixture over the fish and stir lightly until coated. Cover and refrigerate for 15 minutes. Place on a serving platter and garnish with parsley and lemon wedges.

Heat the oil, then pour into the fondue pot. Place over the lit burner. Spear the fish onto the fondue forks and cook for 2 to 3 minutes, then serve with the Sour Cream Sauce, Artichoke & Bean Salad with Vinaigrette, and rice.

Tuna and Tomato Fondue

TUNA & TOMATO FONDUE

THIS FONDUE MAKES A SUBSTANTIAL MEAL WHEN SERVED WITH WARM BREAD OR BAKED POTATOES AND A TOSSED GREEN SALAD.

Serves **4**
Preparation time **10 minutes**
Cooking time **22 to 25 minutes,**
  plus 2 minutes for each piece of tuna

1 lb fresh tuna steak
Fresh basil sprigs
1 Tbsp olive oil
1 small onion, chopped
2 to 3 garlic cloves, peeled and crushed
1 lb ripe tomatoes, skinned
1 Tbsp tomato paste
2 Tbsp water
¹/₂ cup white wine

¹/₂ cup water
Basil sprigs
Salt and freshly ground black pepper
1 red and 1 yellow bell pepper, seeded
  and cubed
1 large zucchini, cubed

TO GARNISH
Basil sprigs.

TO SERVE
Warm crusty bread or potatoes baked in
  their skins, Green Tomatillo Sauce *(see page 100),*
  and Tossed Green Salad *(see page 114).*

Cut the tuna into cubes, place in small bowls with a few basil sprigs, cover, and refrigerate.

Heat the oil in a pan and sauté the onion and garlic for 5 minutes or until softened.

Chop the tomatoes and add to the pan with the tomato paste, blended with 2 tablespoons of water. Cook for 5 minutes then add the wine, water, 2 to 3 sprigs of basil, and seasoning to taste. Bring to a boil, then simmer for 10 to 15 minutes or until a thick sauce is formed.

Purée in a food processor, adjust seasoning, then pour into the fondue pot, and place over the lit burner. Heat through. Dip the bell peppers and zucchini in boiling water, then drain. Arrange in small bowls and garnish with a few basil sprigs.

Spear the tuna and vegetable cubes onto the fondue forks and cook in the tomato sauce. Serve with bread or potatoes, Green Tomatillo Sauce, and the salad.

SEAFOOD & CHEESE FONDUE

USE WHICHEVER SEAFOOD YOU PREFER FOR THIS DELICIOUS CREAMY FONDUE—SHELLFISH GO REALLY
WELL WITH THE CHEESE AND A CRISP, CHILLED CHARDONNAY IS AN EXCELLENT ACCOMPANIMENT.

Place the garlic, chile, and white wine in a pan, bring to a boil, and simmer for 3 minutes. Discard the garlic and chile, pour the wine into the fondue pan, and add the sherry and lime juice. Place over the lit burner.

Mix the cheese and cornstarch together, then gradually add to the fondue pot, stirring continuously until the cheese has melted.

Stir in the chopped scallions and parsley, and heat gently. Spear the fish onto the fondue forks and dip into the fondue until well coated in the cheese and heated through. Garnish with the lemon wedges and serve with the rye bread, dipping sauces, and salads.

Serves **3 to 4**
Preparation time **12 to 15 minutes**
Cooking time **5 to 7 minutes**

1 garlic clove, peeled
1 serrano chile, seeded and chopped
1 cup dry white wine
2 Tbsp dry sherry
1 Tbsp lime juice
1½ cups Emmentaler cheese, grated
1 Tbsp cornstarch
4 scallions, trimmed and chopped
1 Tbsp chopped fresh parsley
1 lb assorted seafish such as cubes of cooked lobster meat, cooked peeled jumbo shrimp, cooked green-lipped mussels, and pieces of smoked mackerel

TO GARNISH
Lemon wedges.

TO SERVE
Rye bread for dipping, Green Tomatillo Sauce *(see page 100)*, Creamy Herb Mayonnaise *(see page 104)*, Chilled Ratatouille *(see page 109)*, and Tossed Green Salad *(see page 114)*.

SHRIMP SATAY FONDUE

THIS RECIPE WOULD ALSO WORK REALLY WELL WITH CUBES OF CHICKEN OR TURKEY, OR A MIXTURE OF ALL THREE—SHRIMP, CHICKEN, AND TURKEY. BE SURE TO SERVE PLENTY OF SATAY SAUCE AS IT IS AN ALL-TIME FAVORITE.

Devein the shrimp, then split along the inner side and flatten to form a butterfly shape. Set aside.

Warm the peanut butter, then gradually stir in the coconut milk to form a creamy sauce. Stir in the garlic, lime, and chiles, and mix lightly. Pour over the shrimp, cover, and leave in the refrigerator for at least 30 minutes. Stir occasionally during marinating.

Heat the oil in the fondue pot, then place on the lit burner.

Drain the shrimp and spear onto fondue forks, then cook in the hot oil for 2 to 3 minutes or until cooked. Serve with the Satay Sauce and salads.

Serves **4**
Preparation time **10 minutes plus 30 minutes marinating time**
Cooking time **2 to 3 minutes per piece**

1 lb raw jumbo shrimp
3 Tbsp smooth or crunchy peanut butter
½ cup coconut milk
2 to 3 garlic cloves, crushed
Grated zest of 1 lime
2 Thai chiles, seeded and chopped
1 pt peanut oil, for frying

TO SERVE

Satay Sauce *(see page 99)*, **Mixed Chinese Green Salad** *(see page 108)*, **and Spiced Rice Salad** *(see page 109)*.

MEAT

CAJUN BEEF FONDUE

DRY SPICE RUBS ARE USED BOTH IN CAJUN AND CARIBBEAN COOKING. YOU CAN INCREASE OR DECREASE THE AMOUNT OF SPICES USED, ACCORDING TO PERSONAL PREFERENCE.

Trim the steak and set aside. Mix together the dry marinade ingredients and rub over the steak. Place on a plate, cover lightly, and leave in the refrigerator for at least 30 minutes.

Heat the oil in the fondue pot to 375°F, then place on the lit burner.

Cut the steak into strips, then thread onto the skewers or fondue forks. Cook in the hot oil for 2 to 5 minutes or until cooked to personal preference.

Garnish with the thyme sprigs, and serve with the Sour Cream Sauce, salad, sweet potatoes, and braised okra.

Serves **4 to 6**
Preparation time **5 minutes plus 30 minutes marinating time**
Cooking time **2 to 5 minutes per strip**

1¼ lbs sirloin steak
¼ tsp dried red pepper flakes
¼ to ½ tsp cayenne pepper
½ tsp sugar
¼ to ½ tsp salt
¼ tsp freshly ground black pepper
2 Tbsp chopped fresh thyme
2 to 3 garlic cloves, peeled and crushed
1 pt oil, for frying

TO GARNISH
Fresh thyme sprigs.

TO SERVE
Sour Cream Sauce *(see page 103)*, **Tossed Green Salad** *(see page 114)*, **caramelized sweet potatoes, and braised okra.**

FONDUE BOURGUIGNONNE

PERHAPS THE MOST WELL KNOWN OF ALL FONDUES, ORIGINATING IN FRANCE, BUT NOW ENJOYED IN MANY DIFFERENT COUNTRIES.

Cut the steak into cubes, place in individual dishes, and garnish with the parsley sprigs and tomato wedges.

Seed and chop the tomatoes into small dice, then place in a small bowl. Place the shallots and parsley in small dishes. Put the garlic clove and bay leaf into the oil, heat the oil in the fondue pot to 375°F, then carefully transfer to the lit burner.

Spear the meat onto the fondue forks and cook in the oil for 1 to 4 minutes, until cooked to personal preference. Once cooked, roll in any or all of the tomatoes, shallots, and parsley. Serve with the creamed horseradish, olives, chutney, dipping sauce, and bread.

Serves **6 to 8**
Preparation time **10 minutes**
Cooking time **1 to 4 minutes per cube**

2 lbs fillet or sirloin steak
4 tomatoes
4 shallots, peeled and chopped
3 Tbsp chopped fresh parsley
1 pt oil, for frying
1 garlic clove, peeled
1 fresh bay leaf

TO GARNISH
Fresh parsley sprigs and tomato wedges.

TO SERVE
Creamed horseradish, olives, fruit chutney, Green Tomatillo Sauce *(see page 100)*, **and crusty bread.**

TURKISH KABOBS FONDUE

SPICES BECOME STALE QUITE QUICKLY SO ALWAYS STORE THEM IN A COOL DARK PLACE. FOR BEST RESULTS, USE THE FRESHEST SPICES AVAILABLE AND GRIND THEM WITH A PESTLE AND MORTAR JUST BEFORE YOU NEED THEM.

Mix together the ground beef, spices, onion, garlic, lemon zest, cilantro, and seasoning to taste. Form into small balls about the size of a cherry tomato. Place on a serving plate, garnish with the cilantro sprigs, and sprinkle with the scallions.

Heat the oil in the fondue pot to 375°F and place carefully on the lit burner.

Spear the meatballs onto fondue forks or skewers, fry in the oil, and serve with the Indian-style Raita and salads.

Serves **4 to 6**
Preparation time **10 minutes**
Cooking time **2 to 5 minutes**
    per meatball

1 lb ground beef
1½ tsp ground coriander
1½ tsp ground cumin
1 small onion, peeled and chopped
3 to 4 garlic cloves, peeled and crushed
1 Tbsp grated lemon zest
2 Tbsp chopped fresh cilantro
Salt and freshly ground black pepper
1 pt oil, for frying

TO GARNISH
Cilantro sprigs and chopped scallions.

TO SERVE
Indian-style Raita *(see page 104)*, Tossed
    Green Salad *(see page 114)*, and Mint and
    Lemon Tabbouleh *(see page 118)*.

SWEET & SOUR BEEF FONDUE

ONE OF THE JOYS IN HOSTING A FONDUE PARTY IS THAT IT CAN BE AS EASY OR AS COMPLICATED AS YOU WISH. MOST OF THIS FONDUE CAN BE PREPARED WELL AHEAD OF TIME: MARINATING THE MEAT OVERNIGHT WILL ENSURE THAT IT WILL SIMPLY MELT IN THE MOUTH. THE BATTER, DIPPING SAUCE, AND SALAD CAN QUICKLY BE MADE JUST BEFORE THEY ARE REQUIRED—THEN ALL YOU HAVE TO DO IS RELAX AND ENJOY THE OCCASION WITH YOUR FRIENDS.

Cut the steak into cubes and place in a shallow dish. Mix together the garlic, sugar, soy sauce, vinegar, and wine, and pour over the meat. Stir and cover. Leave to marinate in the refrigerator for at least 30 minutes, stirring occasionally during marinating.

Mix the eggs and water together until light and frothy, then sift in the flour and cornstarch (do not worry if there are a few lumps). Place in small bowls.

Drain the meat and place in small bowls. Garnish with cilantro sprigs.

Heat the oil to 375°F in the fondue pot, then carefully place on the lit burner. Spear a piece of meat onto a fondue fork, dip in the batter, then fry in the oil until crisp and golden. Serve with the dipping sauce, salad, rice, and mango chutney.

Serves **6**

Preparation time **10 minutes plus 30 minutes marinating time**

Cooking time **2 to 4 minutes per piece**

1½ lbs fillet or sirloin steak
3 to 4 garlic cloves, peeled and crushed
1 Tbsp granulated brown sugar
2 Tbsp soy sauce
2 Tbsp red wine vinegar
1 cup red wine

FOR THE BATTER
2 medium eggs, beaten
1 cup ice-cold water
1 cup all-purpose flour
½ cup cornstarch
1 pt oil, for frying

TO GARNISH
Chopped fresh cilantro.

TO SERVE
Sweet & Sour Sauce *(see page 97)*, Mint & Lemon Tabbouleh *(see page 118)*, fresh cooked rice, and mango chutney.

BEEF IN RED WINE FONDUE

WHEN COOKING WITH WINE, ALWAYS USE THE BEST YOU CAN AFFORD—YOU WILL CERTAINLY NOT REGRET IT.

Serves **6**
Preparation time **8 to 10 minutes**
   plus 30 minutes marinating time
Cooking time **1 to 2 minutes per piece**

2 lbs rump or sirloin steak, trimmed
   and cubed
3 to 5 garlic cloves, peeled and
   sliced fine
4 to 5 shallots, peeled and chopped
1 Tbsp granulated brown sugar
2 Tbsp chopped fresh parsley
1½ cups red wine, such as Bordeaux
1 pt oil, for frying

TO GARNISH
Fresh parsley sprigs.

TO SERVE
Avocado & Mango Salad *(see page 106)*,
   Artichoke Heart Salad *(see page 115)*,
   and crusty bread.

Place the steak in a shallow dish. Scatter over the garlic, shallots, sugar, and parsley, then pour over the red wine. Cover and leave in the refrigerator for at least 30 minutes. Spoon the marinade over the steak occasionally.

When ready to cook, drain the steak, reserving the marinade, and arrange the steak in small dishes. Garnish with parsley sprigs.

Strain, then boil the marinade vigorously for about 10 minutes or until it is reduced by half and has become syrupy. Pour into small dishes and use as a dipping sauce.

Heat the oil to 375°F in the fondue pot then place over the lit burner. Spear the meat onto the fondue forks and cook according to taste. Serve with the salads and bread.

Chile Meatball Fondue

CHILE MEATBALL FONDUE

CHILES CAN VARY TREMENDOUSLY IN BOTH FLAVOR AND HEAT INTENSITY. I HAVE SUGGESTED RED SERRANO CHILES, BECAUSE THEY ARE A PARTICULAR FAVORITE OF MINE. HOWEVER, YOU MAY PREFER TO SUBSTITUTE ANOTHER VARIETY.

Serves **4**
Preparation time **10 minutes**
Cooking time **3 to 5 minutes**
    per meatball

1 lb ground beef
1 small onion, grated
2 to 3 garlic cloves, peeled and crushed
1 to 2 red serrano chiles, seeded and
    chopped fine
1 Tbsp tomato paste
Salt and freshly ground black pepper
1 Tbsp chopped fresh oregano
1 pt oil, for frying

TO GARNISH
Pickled chiles and fresh oregano sprigs.

TO SERVE
Warm pita breads, shredded lettuce,
    and Green Tomatillo Sauce *(see*
    page 100).

Mix together the ground beef, onion, garlic, chiles, tomato paste, seasoning, and chopped oregano. With dampened hands, form into small meatballs the size of a large cherry. Place on a serving plate and garnish with pickled chiles and fresh oregano sprigs.

Heat the oil to 375°F in the fondue pot and place over the lit burner. Spear the meatballs onto fondue forks or skewers and cook in the hot oil for 3 to 5 minutes or until cooked.

Split the pita bread and fill with some shredded lettuce, place the cooked meatballs in the pita, and drizzle with some Green Tomatillo Sauce to serve.

APRICOT & MINT LAMB FONDUE

THIS IS ALSO GOOD SERVED WITH WARM, CRISP TACO SHELLS. SIMPLY FILL THE SHELLS WITH SHREDDED
LETTUCE, AND TOP WITH THE MEATBALLS AND CUCUMBER.

Serves **4 to 6**
Preparation time **10 minutes**
Cooking time **3 to 5 minutes per meatball**

1 lb ground lamb
½ cup ready-to-eat apricots, chopped fine
2 to 3 garlic cloves, peeled and crushed
1 small red onion, chopped fine
2 Tbsp chopped fresh mint
Salt and freshly ground pepper
1 pt oil, for frying

TO GARNISH
Mint sprigs and fresh apricot slices.

TO SERVE
Warm split pita breads, shredded lettuce,
shredded cucumber, Green Mayonnaise *(see page 96)*.

Place the ground lamb with the apricots, garlic, onion, mint, and seasoning in a bowl and mix well. Form into small balls about the size of a small cherry tomato. Place on a plate and garnish with mint sprigs and apricot slices.

Heat the oil in the fondue pot and place over the lit burner. Spear onto the fondue forks or skewers and cook in the hot oil for 3 to 5 minutes or until cooked.

Split the pita breads, fill with lettuce, cucumber, and meatballs, and serve with the mayonnaise.

BEEF & HORSERADISH FONDUE

IF YOU CAN FIND FRESH HORSERADISH, USE IT IN THIS RECIPE BECAUSE THE FLAVOR IS SUPERB. IF NOT, USE SHREDDED OR CREAMED HORSERADISH.

Serves **4**
Preparation time **5 to 7 minutes**
  plus 30 minutes marinating time
Cooking time **2 to 4 minutes per strip**

1¼ lbs sirloin or rump steak
1 to 2 Tbsp grated or creamed horseradish
4 Tbsp olive oil
2 Tbsp red wine vinegar
Salt and freshly ground black pepper
1 pt oil, for frying

TO GARNISH
Flat-leaf parsley.

TO SERVE
Creamed horseradish sauce,
  Sauerkraut *(see page 107)*,
  Creamy Potato and Apple
  Salad *(see page 117)*, and
  crusty bread.

Trim and cut the steak into strips, and place in a shallow dish. Mix together the horseradish, oil, vinegar, and seasoning, then pour over the beef. Stir, cover lightly, and leave to marinate in the refrigerator for at least 30 minutes. Stir occasionally during this time.

Heat the oil in the fondue pot to 375°F, then carefully place over the lit burner. Drain the beef and spear onto the fondue forks. Cook in the hot oil for 2 to 4 minutes or according to personal taste. Garnish with the flat-leaf parsley, and serve with the sauce, salads, and bread.

SICILIAN LAMB FONDUE

WHEN MARINATING FOODS, THE LONGER THE MARINATING TIME, THE BETTER THE FLAVOR. WITH MEAT, LEAVING IT FOR LONGER NOT ONLY IMPROVES THE FLAVOR, BUT ALSO HELPS TO MAKE THE MEAT MORE SUCCULENT.

Cut the lamb into strips and place in a shallow dish. Scatter over the garlic, onion, thyme, spices, and sugar.

Blend the tomato paste, Marsala wine, and lemon juice together and pour over the lamb. Stir, cover, and leave to marinate in the refrigerator for at least 30 minutes, or longer if time permits.

Drain the lamb, reserving the marinade. Arrange the lamb in small dishes, and garnish with the thyme sprigs.

Boil the marinade rapidly until it is reduced by half and has become syrupy, then pour into small dishes and use as a dipping sauce.

Heat the oil in the fondue pot, then place over the lit burner. Thread the lamb onto the fondue forks and cook in the hot oil for 2 to 3 minutes or until cooked to personal preference. Roll in the toasted chopped almonds and serve with the Green Mayonnaise, salads, and bread.

Serves **4 to 6**
Preparation time **8 to 10 minutes plus 30 minutes marinating time**
Cooking time **2 to 3 minutes per piece**

1½ lbs lean lamb fillet
2 to 3 garlic cloves, crushed
1 large onion, chopped
2 Tbsp chopped fresh thyme
1 tsp cumin seeds, toasted
1 tsp ground cardamom
2 Tbsp dark brown sugar
1 Tbsp tomato paste
1 cup Marsala wine
3 Tbsp lemon juice
1 pt oil, for frying

TO GARNISH
Fresh thyme sprigs.

TO SERVE
Toasted chopped sliced almonds, Green Mayonnaise (see page 96), Chilled Ratatouille (see page 109), Spicy Pepper & Mushroom Salad (see page 116), and warm Italian-style bread such as focaccia.

ROSEMARY-SCENTED LAMB FONDUE

LAMB, ROSEMARY, AND GARLIC ARE A WINNING COMBINATION,
AND THE ADDITION OF THE APPLE JUICE ADDS A DELICIOUS TANG.

Serves **6**
Preparation time **10 minutes plus 30 minutes
  marinating time**
Cooking time **2 to 3 minutes per piece**

1½ lbs lean lamb, cut into thin strips
3 to 4 garlic cloves, peeled and crushed
8 scallions, trimmed and chopped
2 Tbsp chopped fresh rosemary
2 Tbsp light soy sauce
1 cup apple juice
1 pt oil, for frying

TO GARNISH
**Rosemary sprigs and wedges of
  dessert apples.**

TO SERVE
Sour Cream Sauce *(see page 103)*,
  Spiced Rice Salad *(see page 109)*,
  Tossed Green Salad *(see page 114)*,
  and crusty bread.

Place the strips of lamb in a shallow dish, then scatter over the garlic, scallions, and rosemary.

Blend the soy sauce with the apple juice, then pour the liquid over the lamb and stir lightly. Cover and leave to marinate in the refrigerator for at least 30 minutes. Stir occasionally.

Heat the oil in the fondue pot and carefully place on the lit burner.

Drain the lamb and boil the marinade vigorously until reduced by half. Serve in small bowls as a dipping sauce.

Thread the lamb onto the fondue forks and cook in the hot oil for 2 to 3 minutes. Garnish with the rosemary and apple wedges, and serve with the Sour Cream Sauce, salads, and crusty bread.

MARINATED PORK & ORANGE FONDUE

MARRYING SAVORY DISHES WITH FRUIT IS A PARTICULAR FAVORITE
OF MINE—AS IN THIS DELICIOUS COMBINATION.

Serves **4**
Preparation time **10 minutes plus
30 minutes marinating time**
Cooking time **3 to 4 minutes per piece**

1 lb pork fillet, cubed
1 medium onion, chopped
1 to 2 garlic cloves, peeled and crushed
2 Tbsp grated orange zest
1/2 cup orange juice
2 tsp granulated brown sugar
1 Tbsp light soy sauce
3 Tbsp walnut oil
2 Tbsp chopped fresh sage
1 pt peanut oil, for frying

TO GARNISH
Fresh sage leaves, orange wedges.

TO SERVE
**Cooked new potatoes, Orange Cumberland
Dipping Sauce *(see page 102)* and Zesty
Orange Coleslaw *(see page 114).***

Place the pork in a shallow dish, then scatter with onion and garlic.

Mix together the orange zest, juice, sugar, soy sauce, walnut oil, and sage, then pour
over the pork. Cover and leave to marinate in the refrigerator for at least 30 minutes.

Drain the pork, reserving the marinade, and place the pork in individual dishes
garnished with the sage leaves and orange wedges.

Boil the marinade rapidly until reduced by half, pour into small bowls, and serve as a
dipping sauce. Heat the oil in the fondue pot, then carefully place over the lit burner.
Spear the pork onto fondue forks and cook in the hot oil. Serve with the potatoes,
Orange Cumberland Dipping Sauce, and coleslaw.

Marinated Pork & Orange Fondue

ASIAN FRUITY PORK FONDUE

YOU CAN BUY DIFFERENT TYPES OF MANGO CHUTNEY—SOME ARE MILD WHILE OTHERS HAVE QUITE A BITE TO THEM. CHOOSE WHICHEVER YOU PREFER, BUT CHOP THE LARGER PIECES OF CHUTNEY BEFORE USING.

Place the ground pork in a bowl and add the mango chutney, chiles, garlic, shallots, and cilantro. Mix together then form into small balls about the size of a large cherry. Place on a serving platter and garnish with the mango and pineapple, and the chopped cilantro.

Heat the oil in the fondue pot, then carefully transfer to the lit burner. Spear the meatballs onto skewers or fondue forks and cook in the heated oil for 3 to 5 minutes or until cooked.

Serve with the glutinous (short-grain) rice, Sweet & Sour Sauce, pineapple, bell peppers, and mango chutney.

Serves **6**
Preparation time **10 minutes**
Cooking time **3 to 5 minutes**
  per meatball

1$\frac{1}{2}$ **lbs ground pork**
3 Tbsp mango chutney
2 jalapeño chiles, peeled and chopped fine
2 to 3 garlic cloves, peeled and crushed
4 shallots, peeled and chopped
2 Tbsp chopped fresh cilantro
1 pt peanut oil, for frying

TO GARNISH
Slices of fresh mango and pineapple,
  and fresh chopped cilantro.

TO SERVE
Glutinous (short-grain) rice, Sweet & Sour
  Sauce *(see page 97)*, **fresh chopped**
  pineapple, fresh chopped green and
  red bell peppers, and mango chutney.

PORK & PEANUT FONDUE

USE EITHER SMOOTH OR CHUNKY PEANUT BUTTER TO MARINATE THE PORK; THE CHOICE IS YOURS. WARMING THE PEANUT BUTTER FIRST MAKES IT EASIER TO BLEND WITH THE OTHER INGREDIENTS.

Cut the pork fillet into thin strips and place in a shallow dish. Blend the peanut butter with the chile, garlic, sugar, soy sauce, lemon juice, and peanut oil. Pour over the pork, stir, cover, and leave to marinate in the refrigerator for at least 30 minutes.

Heat the oil in the fondue pot, then carefully place over the lit burner.

Drain the pork, thread onto skewers, and cook in the hot oil for 3 to 4 minutes or until cooked. Garnish with the lime or lemon wedges, and chopped cilantro, and serve with the Satay Sauce and salad.

Serves **4**

Preparation time **8 to 10 minutes plus 30 minutes marinating time**

Cooking time **3 to 4 minutes per strip**

1 lb pork fillet

4 Tbsp peanut butter

1 red serrano chile, seeded and chopped

2 to 3 garlic cloves, peeled and crushed

2 tsp dark granulated brown sugar

1 Tbsp soy sauce

2 Tbsp lemon juice

2 Tbsp peanut oil

1 pt oil, for frying

TO GARNISH

Lime or lemon wedges, and chopped cilantro.

TO SERVE

Satay Sauce *(see page 99)*, and Mixed Chinese Green Salad *(see page 108)*.

APPLE PORK FONDUE

CALVADOS APPLE BRANDY COMES FROM NORMANDY, FRANCE, AND HAS A VERY DISTINCTIVE FLAVOR. IT IS WELL WORTH BUYING IF YOU GET THE OPPORTUNITY. IF IT IS NOT AVAILABLE, SUBSTITUTE ANOTHER GOOD-QUALITY BRANDY.

Cut the pork into cubes and place in a shallow dish. Scatter over the scallions, pepper, and sage, then mix the Calvados and apple juice, and pour over. Stir lightly, cover, and leave to marinate in the refrigerator for at least 30 minutes. Stir occasionally.

Heat the oil in the fondue pot and carefully place over the lit burner. Drain the pork and spear with fondue forks.

Cook in the hot oil for 2 to 5 minutes or until cooked. Garnish with the apple wedges and serve with the pasta, sage with black pepper, mayonnaise, salad, and bread.

Serves **4 to 6**
Preparation time **5 to 7 minutes plus 30 minutes marinating time**
Cooking time **2 to 5 minutes per cube**

1¼ lbs pork tenderloin
6 scallions, trimmed and chopped
Freshly ground black pepper
2 Tbsp chopped fresh sage
3 Tbsp Calvados
½ cup apple juice
1 pt oil, for frying

TO GARNISH
Apple wedges.

TO SERVE
Fresh cooked tagliatelle tossed in butter, chopped sage with black pepper, Creamy Herb Mayonnaise (see page 104), **Tossed Green Salad** (see page 114), **and crusty bread.**

POULTRY

MONGOLIAN CHICKEN HOT POT

THESE HOT POT FONDUES ARE ALSO KNOWN AS ASIAN FONDUES. THE POTS ARE SOMETIMES REFERRED TO AS CHRYSANTHEMUM POTS, DUE TO THE DECORATIVE PATTERN ON THE BASE, AND THE WAY THE FLAMES FROM THE BURNER CREATE A WONDERFUL PATTERN IN THE SHAPE OF A CHRYSANTHEMUM.

Cut the chicken into thin strips and place in shallow dishes, cover lightly, and store in the refrigerator until required.

Place the broth in the Mongolian hot pot or fondue pot. Add the chiles, gingerroot, garlic, shallots, star anise, and honey. Bring to a boil, then simmer for 10 minutes. Place over the lit burner.

Meanwhile, cut the zucchini into thin strips. Seed the peppers and cut into thin strips. Place the zucchini and peppers in boiling water for 5 minutes, then drain. Arrange on serving dishes. Garnish the chicken and vegetables with the cilantro.

Mix the ingredients for the dipping sauce together and pour into small bowls.

Spear the chicken and the vegetable strips onto the forks and cook in the hot broth for 2 to 4 minutes. When all the chicken and vegetables have been cooked, add the bean sprouts to the broth. Heat for 2 minutes and serve the broth as a soup, garnished with the chopped red chiles.

Serves **6 to 8**
Preparation time **15 minutes**
Cooking time **2 to 4 minutes per strip**

2 lbs chicken breast
1 pt chicken broth
2 Thai chiles, seeded and crushed
1 Tbsp grated ginger root
3 to 4 garlic cloves, peeled and crushed
4 shallots, peeled and chopped
4 star anise
2 to 3 tsp liquid honey
2 medium zucchini
1 red bell pepper
1 yellow bell pepper
1 cup bean sprouts

FOR THE DIPPING SAUCE
3 Tbsp light soy sauce
1 tsp liquid honey
½ tsp crushed dried chiles
2 tsp dry sherry

TO GARNISH
Chopped cilantro and chopped red chiles.

CHICKEN & CHILE MEATBALL FONDUE

THIS RECIPE CALLS FOR TOASTED CUMIN SEEDS, WHICH CAN BE DONE IN THREE WAYS: PLACE ON A COOKIE SHEET AND COOK IN A HOT OVEN FOR ABOUT 10 MINUTES, SHAKING THE TRAY OCCASIONALLY; OR PLACE ON A FOIL-LINED BROILER PAN AND BROIL UNDER A MODERATE HEAT FOR 2 TO 3 MINUTES; OR SPRINKLE IN A SKILLET AND HEAT GENTLY, STIRRING FOR 2 TO 3 MINUTES. TAKE CARE NOT TO BURN THE SEEDS BECAUSE THIS WILL IMPAIR THE FLAVOR.

Serves **4**
Preparation time **15 to 20 minutes including**
  toasting the cumin seeds
Cooking time **3 to 4 minutes per piece**

1 lb ground chicken
2 to 3 jalapeño chiles, seeded and chopped
1 tsp toasted cumin seeds
1 small onion, peeled and chopped
2 to 3 garlic cloves, crushed
Salt and freshly ground black pepper
2 Tbsp chopped fresh thyme
1 pt oil, for frying

TO GARNISH
Sprigs of thyme.

TO SERVE
Green Mayonnaise *(see page 96)*, **Indian-style**
  Raita *(see page 101)*, **Artichoke & Bean**
  Salad with Vinaigrette *(see page 110)*,
  and crusty bread.

Mix together the ground chicken with the
chiles, cumin seeds, onion, garlic, seasoning,
and thyme. Form into small balls. Place in a
serving bowl and garnish with the thyme.
Cover lightly and refrigerate.

Heat the oil in the fondue pot to 350°F,
then carefully transfer to the lit burner.

Spear the meatballs onto the fondue fork
and cook in the hot oil for 3 to 4 minutes.

Serve with the Green Mayonnaise, Indian-style
Raita, Artichoke & Bean Salad with
Vinaigrette, and bread.

SMOKY CHICKEN FONDUE

A VARIETY OF DRIED CHILES IS AVAILABLE, VARYING FROM
AROMATIC, SMOKY FLAVORS TO FRUITY. FOR THIS FONDUE,
I WOULD RECOMMEND USING MULATOS OR CHIPOTLES.

Serves **4 to 6**
Preparation time **18 minutes,**
  plus 30 minutes marinating time
Cooking time **2 to 4 minutes per cube**

1 to 2 dried chiles
1¼ lbs boneless chicken breast
4 to 5 whole cloves
1 tsp ground cinnamon
2 Tbsp white wine vinegar
1 Tbsp tomato paste
1 Tbsp Worcestershire sauce
1 pt oil, for frying

TO GARNISH
Pickled chiles and cilantro sprigs.

TO SERVE
Green Tomatillo Sauce *(see page 100)*,
  Sour Cream Sauce *(see page 103)*,
  Spiced Rice Salad *(see page 109)*,
  and crusty bread.

Dry fry the chiles in a skillet for 2 to 3 minutes, remove from the heat, and
place in a small bowl. Cover with 1 cup of very hot (but not boiling) water
and leave for at least 10 minutes. Drain, reserving the liquor, and chop fine.

Cut the chicken into cubes and sprinkle the chiles, cloves, and cinnamon over
the cubes. Blend the vinegar with the tomato paste, Worcestershire sauce, and
chile soaking liquor, then pour over the chicken.

Cover lightly, then leave to marinate in the refrigerator for at least 30 minutes.
Stir occasionally during marinating. Heat the oil in the fondue pot to 350°F and
carefully place over the lit burner.

Drain the chicken, arrange in small bowls, and garnish with pickled chiles and
cilantro sprigs. Thread the chicken onto the fondue forks and cook in the hot
oil for 2 to 4 minutes. Serve with the Green Tomatillo Sauce, Sour Cream
Sauce, Spiced Rice Salad, and bread.

SOUTHERN CHICKEN FONDUE

THESE TENDER, SUCCULENT STRIPS OF CHICKEN ARE COATED
IN A LIGHT BATTER THEN QUICKLY FRIED.

Serves **4 to 6**
Preparation time **10 minutes plus**
  30 minutes marinating time
Cooking time **3 to 4 minutes per strip**

1¼ lbs chicken breast, cut into strips
4 Tbsp orange juice
1 red serrano chile, seeded and crushed
2 to 3 garlic cloves, peeled and crushed
2 Tbsp chopped fresh parsley

FOR THE BATTER
1 cup all-purpose flour
2 Tbsp cornmeal

½ tsp black pepper
1 tsp hot paprika
1 medium egg, beaten
¾ cup milk
1 pt oil, for frying

TO GARNISH
Parsley sprigs and wedges
  of tomato.

TO SERVE
Corn relish, corn fritters,
  and cornbread.

Place the chicken in a shallow dish. Mix the orange juice, chile, garlic, and parsley together and pour over the chicken. Stir, cover lightly, and refrigerate for at least 30 minutes.

Meanwhile, make the batter by sifting the flours into a mixing bowl, then stir in the peppers. Make a well in the center and add the egg. Gradually add the milk, drawing the flour in from the sides of the bowl to form a smooth batter. Leave to stand for 30 minutes, then stir well just before using.

Heat the oil to 350°F in the fondue pot and carefully place over the lit burner. Place the chicken into serving bowls; garnish with parsley and tomato.

Thread the chicken onto fondue forks, dip into the batter, and cook in the hot oil for 3 to 4 minutes. Serve with corn relish, corn fritters, and cornbread.

Caribbean Chicken Fondue

CARIBBEAN CHICKEN FONDUE

THESE DAYS THE AVAILABILITY OF MANY DIVERSE FOODS MAKES IT EASY FOR US TO ENJOY THE BEST OF ALL CUISINES, AS CAN BE SEEN IN THIS RECIPE FROM THE SUNNY CARIBBEAN.

Serves **6**
Preparation time **5 to 7 minutes**
   plus 30 minutes marinating time
Cooking time **2 to 4 minutes per piece**

2 lbs chicken breast, cut into cubes
2 Tbsp brown sugar
1 to 3 Scotch bonnet chiles, seeded and
   chopped fine
3 to 4 garlic cloves, peeled and crushed
2 Tbsp chopped fresh cilantro
1 cup mango juice
1 pt oil, for frying

TO GARNISH
Mango wedges and pickled chiles.

TO SERVE
Green Tomatillo Sauce *(see page 100)*, **Artichoke Heart Salad** *(see page 115)*, **cooked rice or cornbread.**

Place the chicken in a shallow dish. Sprinkle with the sugar, chiles, garlic, and cilantro, then pour over the mango juice. Stir lightly, then cover and leave to marinate in the refrigerator for at least 30 minutes. Stir occasionally.

Heat the oil in the fondue pot to 350°F then carefully place over the lit burner.

Drain the chicken, boil the marinade vigorously for 10 minutes or until reduced by half, then pour into small bowls, and use as a dipping sauce.

Place the chicken in small bowls and garnish with the mango wedges and pickled chiles.

Spear the chicken onto the fondue forks then cook in the hot oil for 2 to 4 minutes or until cooked. Serve with the Green Tomatillo Sauce, Artichoke Heart Salad, and rice or cornbread.

SIZZLING TURKEY FONDUE

THIS FONDUE IS BASED ON THE EVER-POPULAR MEXICAN SIZZLING
FAJITAS. BE SURE THE TURKEY IS WELL COOKED.

Serves **4**
Preparation time **8 to 10 minutes plus
 30 minutes marinating time**
Cooking time **2 to 4 minutes per piece**

$1\frac{1}{4}$ **lbs turkey breast, cut into strips**
**2 to 3 serrano chiles, seeded and chopped
or $\frac{1}{2}$ to 1 tsp crushed dried chiles**
6 scallions, chopped
3 to 4 garlic cloves, crushed
2 Tbsp chopped fresh cilantro
2 tsp warmed liquid honey

3 Tbsp lime juice
6 Tbsp olive oil
1 pt oil, for frying

TO GARNISH
Lime wedges.

TO SERVE
Guacamole, Salsa *(see page 99),*
 Sour Cream Sauce *(see page 103),*
 **shredded scallions, and warmed
 tortilla pancakes.**

Place the turkey strips in a shallow dish. Scatter over the chiles, scallions,
garlic, and cilantro. Mix together the honey, lime juice, and olive oil,
and pour over the turkey. Stir, cover, and marinate in the refrigerator for
at least 30 minutes.

Heat the oil to 375°F in the fondue pot then carefully transfer to the lit burner.

Drain the turkey, arrange on serving plates, and garnish with the lime. Spear
the turkey onto the fondue forks and cook in the hot oil for 2 to 4 minutes.

Serve with the guacamole, Salsa, sauce, scallions, and pancakes.

Sizzling Turkey Fondue

PACIFIC RIM FONDUE

HERE I HAVE COMBINED EASTERN FLAVORS WITH A WESTERN COOKING METHOD—THE RESULT IS DELICIOUS!

Serves **6 to 8**
Preparation time **10 minutes plus 30 minutes marinating time**
Cooking time **2 to 4 minutes per cube**

2 lbs chicken breast, cut into cubes
1 Tbsp grated lime zest
2 Thai chiles, seeded and chopped
3 garlic cloves, peeled and crushed
2 Tbsp grated gingerroot
6 scallions, chopped
2 Tbsp chopped fresh cilantro
4 Tbsp lime juice

3 Tbsp olive oil
1 Tbsp sesame oil
1 pt oil, for frying

TO GARNISH
Scallions and cilantro sprigs.

TO SERVE
Sweet & Sour Sauce *(see page 97)*, **Spicy Pepper & Mushroom Salad** *(see page 116)*, **and Creamy Potato & Apple Salad** *(see page 117)*.

Place the chicken in a shallow dish. Scatter over the lime zest, chiles, garlic, gingerroot, scallions, and cilantro. Blend the lime juice with the oils and pour over the chicken. Stir, then cover and refrigerate for at least 30 minutes.

Drain the chicken and place in small bowls, garnished with the scallions and cilantro.

Heat the oil in the fondue pot to 350°F then place over the lit burner. Spear the chicken onto the fondue forks and cook in the hot oil for 2 to 4 minutes or until cooked.

Serve with Sweet & Sour Sauce, Spicy Pepper & Mushroom Salad, and Creamy Potato & Apple Salad.

HOT 'N' SPICY TURKEY FONDUE

MAKE THIS DISH AS HOT AND FIERY AS YOU DARE, SIMPLY BY INCREASING THE AMOUNT OR VARIETY OF CHILES USED, AND—FOR THE REALLY BRAVE—KEEPING THE SEEDS AND MEMBRANE IN THE CHILES.

Cut the turkey into strips and place in a shallow dish. Mix together the chiles, garlic, Tabasco Sauce, cilantro, honey, lime juice, and the 6 tablespoons of oil, and pour over the turkey. Cover and leave to marinate in the refrigerator for at least 30 minutes. Drain and arrange in small bowls, and garnish with cilantro sprigs, pickled chiles, and tomato wedges.

Heat the pint of oil to 375°F in the fondue pot and carefully place on the lit burner. Thread the turkey strips onto the fondue forks or skewers and cook in the hot oil for 2 to 4 minutes.

Serve with the tortilla pancakes, lettuce, scallions, Salsa, and Sour Cream Sauce.

Serves **6 to 8**
Preparation time **8 to 10 minutes plus 30 minutes marinating time**
Cooking time **2 to 4 minutes per strip**

2 lbs turkey breast
2 to 3 chiles, seeded and chopped
3 to 4 garlic cloves, peeled and chopped
2 to 3 tsp Tabasco Sauce
2 Tbsp chopped fresh cilantro
2 tsp warmed liquid honey
3 Tbsp lime juice
6 Tbsp oil
1 pt oil, for frying

TO GARNISH

Cilantro sprigs, pickled chiles, tomato wedges.

TO SERVE

Warmed tortilla pancakes, shredded lettuce, shredded scallions, Salsa *(see page 99)*, **and Sour Cream Sauce** *(see page 103)*.

TURKEY & SATAY FONDUE

IF YOU ARE WEIGHT-CONSCIOUS, THIS FONDUE IS IDEAL, AS TURKEY IS VERY LOW IN FAT—LOWER IN FAT THAN CHICKEN. THE TURKEY IS MARINATED IN LOW-FAT YOGURT AND QUICKLY FRIED AND DRAINED.

Cut the turkey breast into strips and place in a shallow dish. Blend together the yogurt, peanut butter, orange zest and juice, chile, and grated gingerroot. Pour over the turkey and stir. Cover and leave to marinate in the refrigerator for at least 30 minutes. Stir occasionally during marinating.

Heat the oil to 375°F in the fondue pot and carefully place on the lit burner.

Thread the turkey onto the fondue forks and cook in the hot oil for 2 to 4 minutes. Drain on paper towels if preferred. Garnish with the orange wedges, flat-leaf parsley, and chile, and serve with the Satay Sauce, Spiced Rice Salad, and bread.

Serves **4 to 6**
Preparation time **10 minutes plus
30 minutes marinating time**
Cooking time **2 to 4 minutes
per strip**

1¼ lbs turkey breast
6 Tbsp low-fat, plain yogurt
3 Tbsp smooth or chunky peanut
    butter, warmed
2 Tbsp grated orange zest
4 Tbsp orange juice
1 Thai chile, seeded and chopped
1 Tbsp grated fresh gingerroot
1 pt oil, for frying

TO GARNISH
**Orange wedges, flat-leaf parsley,
and chopped red chile.**

TO SERVE
Satay Sauce *(see page 99)*,
    Spiced Rice Salad *(see page 109)*,
    and crusty bread.

CRISPY TURKEY FONDUE

LITTLE MORSELS OF TURKEY, DELICATELY FLAVORED WITH MINT AND LEMON, WILL MAKE THIS FONDUE POPULAR WITH ALL.

Mix together the ground turkey, chopped mint, lemon zest, onion, and garlic, with seasoning to taste. Form into small balls.

Place the beaten egg into a shallow dish and the bread crumbs in a separate dish. Dip the turkey balls in the egg, allowing any excess to drip back into the bowl, then coat in the bread crumbs. Arrange on serving plates and garnish with lemon wedges and mint sprigs. Chill, lightly covered, until required.

Heat the oil in the fondue pot to 350°F, then carefully transfer to the lit burner. Cook the turkey balls in the oil for 3 to 5 minutes, or until they are cooked.

Serve with the Sweet & Sour Sauce, Chilled Ratatouille, Zesty Orange Coleslaw, and new potatoes.

Serves **4 to 6**
Preparation time **10 minutes**
Cooking time **3 to 5 minutes per piece**

1 lb fresh ground turkey
2 Tbsp chopped fresh mint
2 Tbsp grated lemon zest
1 small onion, peeled and grated
2 to 3 garlic cloves, peeled and crushed
Salt and freshly ground black pepper
1 medium egg, beaten
¾ cup dried bread crumbs
1 pt oil, for frying

TO GARNISH
Lemon wedges and mint sprigs.

TO SERVE
Sweet & Sour Sauce *(see page 97)*,
　Chilled Ratatouille *(see page 109)*,
　Zesty Orange Coleslaw *(see page 114)*,
　and freshly cooked new potatoes.

LEMON TURKEY FONDUE

MARINATING THE TURKEY IN THE LEMON JUICE AND CORNSTARCH MAKES IT MELT IN THE MOUTH. TRY FOR YOURSELF AND SEE.

Cut the turkey into cubes and place in a shallow dish. Mix together the lemon zest and juice, olive oil, cornstarch, chiles, and soy sauce. Pour over the turkey and stir lightly. Cover and leave to marinate in the refrigerator for at least 30 minutes. Stir occasionally during marinating.

Drain the turkey, place in serving bowls, and garnish with the lemon wedges and parsley sprigs.

Heat the oil to 350°F in the fondue pot and carefully place over a lit burner. Spear the turkey cubes with fondue forks and cook in the hot oil for 2 to 4 minutes, or until cooked.

Serve with the Blue Cheese Dressing, Green Mayonnaise, Tossed Green Salad, and glutinous rice.

Serves **6 to 8**
Preparation time **8 minutes plus 30 minutes marinating time**
Cooking time **2 to 4 minutes per cube**

2 lbs turkey breast
2 Tbsp grated lemon zest
6 Tbsp lemon juice
2 Tbsp olive oil
3 Tbsp cornstarch
1 to 2 tsp crushed dried chiles
2 Tbsp light soy sauce
1 pt oil, for frying

TO GARNISH
Lemon wedges and flat-leaf parsley sprigs.

TO SERVE
Blue Cheese Dressing *(see page 96)*, **Green Mayonnaise** *(see page 96)*, **Tossed Green Salad** *(see page 114)*, **and cooked glutinous (short-grain) rice.**

MARINATED DUCK FONDUE

IF POSSIBLE, USE BARBARY DUCK FOR THIS RECIPE. THE BREASTS ARE PLUMP AND FULL OF FLAVOR, WHICH IS SEALED IN BY COOKING QUICKLY IN HOT OIL.

Remove the skin and any fat from the duck. Cut into thin strips, and place in a shallow dish.

Gently warm the marmalade, then stir in the orange juice, sage, and walnut oil. Pour over the duck breast, stir, then cover and leave to marinate in the refrigerator for at least 30 minutes. Stir occasionally during marinating.

Heat the oil in the fondue pot to 350°F, and carefully place over the lit burner.

Drain the duck and place in a serving bowl. Garnish with the strips of orange peel and sage leaves.

Spear the duck strips onto the fondue forks or skewers and cook in the hot oil for 2 to 4 minutes or until cooked.

Serve with the Sweet & Sour Sauce, Orange Cumberland Dipping Sauce, Artichoke Heart Salad, and new potatoes.

Serves **4**
Preparation time **10 minutes plus**
   30 minutes marinating time
Cooking time **2 to 4 minutes per strip**

3 to 4 duck breasts, depending on size
4 Tbsp orange marmalade
3 Tbsp orange juice
2 Tbsp chopped fresh sage
2 Tbsp walnut oil
1 pt oil, for frying

TO GARNISH
Fine strips of orange peel and sage leaves.

TO SERVE
Sweet & Sour Sauce *(see page 97)***,**
   Orange Cumberland Dipping Sauce
   *(see page 102)***, Artichoke Heart Salad**
   *(see page 115)***, and freshly cooked**
   new potatoes.

RED DUCK FONDUE

LIKE STEAK, DUCK BREAST CAN BE EATEN EITHER RARE OR WELL DONE.

Serves **4**
Preparation time **10 minutes**
  plus **30 minutes marinating time**
Cooking time **2 to 4 minutes**
  per piece

3 to 4 duck breasts, according to size
4 Tbsp plum jam
2 Tbsp lemon juice
1 tsp dried crushed chiles
1 Tbsp granulated dark brown sugar
1 Tbsp soy sauce
1 pt oil, for frying

TO GARNISH

Ripe plum slices and
  flat-leaf parsley sprigs.

TO SERVE

Orange Cumberland Dipping
  Sauce *(see page 102)*,
  Spiced Rice Salad *(see
  page 109)*, Artichoke &
  Bean Salad with
  Vinaigrette *(see page 110)*.

Discard the skin and fat from the duck breasts and cut into thin strips. Place in a shallow dish.

Warm the jam, then stir in the lemon juice, chiles, sugar, and soy sauce. Pour over the duck breasts, stir, cover, and leave to marinate in the refrigerator for at least 30 minutes. Stir occasionally during marinating.

Heat the oil in the fondue pot to 350°F, then carefully place over the lit burner.

Drain the duck and spear onto fondue forks or skewers. Cook in the hot oil for 2 to 4 minutes .

Garnish with the plum slices and parsley, and serve with Orange Cumberland Dipping Sauce, Spiced Rice Salad, and Artichoke & Bean Salad with Vinaigrette.

DUCK & TOMATILLOS FONDUE

TOMATILLOS CAN BE BOUGHT FRESH OR CANNED.

Serves **4**
Preparation time **10 to 12 minutes**
  plus **30 minutes marinating time**
Cooking time **2 to 4 minutes**
  per cube

3 to 4 duck breasts, depending on size
1½ cups tomatillos or green
  tomatoes, seeded and chopped
2 Fresno chiles, seeded and chopped
1 small onion, chopped
2 to 3 garlic cloves, crushed
1 Tbsp grated lemon zest, optional
2 Tbsp chopped fresh cilantro
5 Tbsp olive oil
2 Tbsp balsamic vinegar
1 pt oil, for frying

TO GARNISH

Cilantro sprigs and lemon
  wedges.

TO SERVE

Salsa *(see page 99)*, Spicy
  Pepper & Mushroom
  Salad *(see page 116)*, and
  warm tortilla pancakes.

Skin the duck breasts, cut into cubes, and place in a shallow dish. Place the chopped tomatillos or tomatoes in a food processor with the chiles, onion, garlic, and lemon zest if using. Blend to a purée. Stir in the cilantro, olive oil, and balsamic vinegar, then pour over the duck. Stir until coated. Cover, and leave to marinate in the refrigerator for at least 30 minutes. Stir occasionally.

Heat the oil to 350°F in the fondue pot, and carefully place over the lit burner. Drain the duck and spear with fondue forks or skewers. Cook in the hot oil for 2 to 4 minutes.

Garnish with cilantro and lemon wedges, and serve with the Salsa, Spicy Pepper & Mushroom Salad, and tortilla pancakes.

CHEESE

TRADITIONAL SWISS FONDUE

REPUTED TO BE THE ORIGINAL OF ALL CHEESE FONDUES, THIS IS NOW THE NATIONAL DISH OF SWITZERLAND. MAKE SURE YOU BUY GENUINE SWISS GRUYÈRE AND EMMENTALER CHEESE, AS THEY ARE LESS LIKELY TO "LUMP" THAN OTHER VARIETIES.

Cut the garlic clove, then rub it around the inside of the fondue pot. Pour in the wine and lemon juice, and place over the lit burner. Gradually add the cheeses, stirring throughout until completely melted.

When the cheese has melted and begins to bubble, blend the cornstarch with the kirsch and stir into the pot. Cook, stirring, for 2 to 3 minutes. Add remaining ingredients to taste, then serve with the Tossed Green Salad, cubes of French bread to dip into the fondue, and pear slices to freshen the palate.

Serves **4**
Preparation time **10 minutes**
Cooking time **10 to 12 minutes**

1 garlic clove
⅔ cup dry white wine
Squeeze of lemon juice
2 cups grated Gruyère cheese
2 cups grated Emmentaler cheese
1 Tbsp cornstarch

2 Tbsp kirsch
Pinch of salt
¼ tsp paprika
¼ tsp grated nutmeg

TO SERVE
Tossed Green Salad *(see page 114)*, **cubes of French bread for dipping, and fresh ripe pear slices.**

BRIE & LOBSTER FONDUE

THIS FONDUE IS DEFINITELY ONE FOR WHEN YOU ARE OUT TO IMPRESS. IT IS WICKEDLY CREAMY AND FOR EVEN GREATER ENJOYMENT YOU CAN SERVE IT WITH FRESHLY COOKED SCALLOPS, DUBLIN BAY PRAWNS, ASPARAGUS SPEARS, BREAD STICKS, AND PRETZELS.

Melt the butter in the fondue pot and gently sauté the shallots for 10 minutes, or until softened but not colored. Sprinkle in the flour and cook for a further 2 minutes.

Gradually add the broth, stirring throughout until the mixture thickens, then simmer for 4 minutes.

Discard any unwanted rind from the Brie and cut into cubes. Stir into the fondue with the cream. Continue to cook, stirring until the mixture is smooth.

Stir in the flaked lobster meat with the lemon juice, Tabasco Sauce, black pepper, and paprika, and heat through.

Carefully place over the lit burner, stir in the chopped parsley, and serve with the dippers and salads.

Serves **4**
Preparation time **10 minutes**
Cooking time **22 to 25 minutes**

¼ **stick butter**
4 shallots, peeled and chopped
2 Tbsp white all-purpose flour
1½ **cups fish or chicken broth**
2 cups ripe French Brie
⅔ **cup heavy cream**
8 oz cooked lobster meat, flaked
2 Tbsp lemon juice
Tabasco Sauce to taste
Freshly ground black pepper
1 tsp paprika
1 Tbsp chopped fresh parsley

TO SERVE

Freshly cooked scallops, Dublin Bay prawns, blanched asparagus spears, bread sticks, and pretzels for dipping. Tossed Green Salad *(see page 114)* **and Artichoke Heart Salad** *(see page 115).*

DEVILED CRAB & CHEESE FONDUE

USE FRESH CRABMEAT IF YOU CAN, AS THE FLAVOR IS FAR SUPERIOR TO THAT OF CANNED OR FROZEN. IF FRESH CRABMEAT IS NOT AVAILABLE, USE A LITTLE EXTRA TABASCO SAUCE TO HELP DEVELOP THE FLAVOR OF THE FONDUE.

Serves **4**
Preparation time **8 to 10 minutes**
Cooking time **7 to 9 minutes**

$2/3$ **cup dry white wine**
3 cups grated Gruyère cheese
1 cup crumbled Roquefort cheese
$1/4$ **cup Boursin Natural cheese**
1 Tbsp cornstarch
1 tsp dry mustard powder
8 oz white crabmeat, flaked
$1/4$ **to** $1/2$ **tsp Tabasco Sauce**
1 Tbsp lemon juice
4 scallions, chopped

TO SERVE
Crusty bread, cooked jumbo shrimp, wedges of cucumber, chicory leaves for dipping, and the Artichoke & Bean Salad with Vinaigrette (see page 110).

Pour the wine into the fondue pot and heat gently, then carefully place over the lit burner.

Toss the cheeses in the cornstarch and add the mustard powder. Gradually add to the wine, stirring continuously. When all the cheese has been added, stir in the crabmeat with the Tabasco Sauce, lemon juice, and scallions. Heat gently, stirring throughout until thick, then serve with the dippers and salad.

CALIFORNIAN FONDUE

HERE I HAVE USED A BLUSH WINE FROM THE NAPA VALLEY. LOOK FOR ONE THAT IS ON THE DRY SIDE RATHER THAN SWEET. THE USE OF BLUSH WINE GIVES THE FONDUE A WONDERFUL ROSY COLOR, BEAUTIFULLY OFFSET BY THE PINK OF THE SHRIMP.

Serves **4**
Preparation time **10 minutes**
Cooking time **10 minutes**

1 garlic clove
$2/3$ **cup blush wine**
3 cups grated Gruyère cheese
1 Tbsp cornstarch
1 Tbsp kirsch
$2/3$ **cup sour cream**
$1/4$ **tsp grated nutmeg**
Freshly ground black pepper
$2/3$ **cup cooked shrimp, peeled and chopped**
2 Tbsp freshly chopped chives

TO SERVE
Natural cubes of challah bread, wedges of pineapple, melon, ripe pears, and apples for dipping. Zesty Orange Coleslaw (see page 114) and Spicy Pepper & Mushroom Salad (see page 116).

Cut the garlic and rub on the insides of the fondue pot. Pour in the wine and heat gently. Place over the lit burner.

Toss the cheese in the cornstarch then gradually add to the wine and heat gently, stirring continuously until melted.

Stir in the kirsch, sour cream, nutmeg, and black pepper to taste. Continue to cook until thickened, then stir in the chopped shrimp and chives. Heat through for 2 to 3 minutes before serving with the dippers and salads.

STILTON FONDUE

STILTON IS A STRONG CHEESE AND THEREFORE NEEDS THE STRONG FLAVORS OF LAGER, MUSTARD, AND PAPRIKA TO ACCOMPANY IT. FOR SOMETHING A LITTLE DIFFERENT, SERVE THE STILTON WITH FRESH OR DRIED APRICOTS.

Heat the lager in the fondue pot then carefully place over the lit burner.

Toss the cheeses in the cornstarch and gradually stir into the lager, stirring continuously. When all the cheese has been added, stir in the mustard and paprika, and continue to heat gently until thick and creamy.

Serve with the dippers and salads.

Serves **4**
Preparation time **10 minutes**
Cooking time **10 minutes**

1 cup lager
3 cups crumbled blue Stilton cheese
1 cup grated Monterey Jack cheese
2 Tbsp cornstarch
1 tsp whole-grain mustard
1 tsp hot paprika

TO SERVE
Baby button mushrooms, apple wedges, large red Flame Tokay and seedless white grapes, and wedges of melon for dipping. Chunks of blue Stilton, Mediterranean Salad *(see page 112)*, and Spicy Pepper & Mushroom Salad *(see page 116)*.

SMOKY BACON & CHEESE FONDUE

THE INFORMALITY OF A FONDUE PARTY MEANS IT IS AN IDEAL WAY OF INTRODUCING PEOPLE TO EACH OTHER. CONVERSATION FLOWS FREELY WHILE EVERYONE DIPS INTO THE FONDUE POT. FONDUE PARTIES ARE ALSO EASY ON THE HOSTS, AS THEY CAN JOIN IN AND NOT BE FOREVER CHECKING ON THE FOOD.

Heat the butter in a small pan and sauté the garlic and shallots for 5 minutes, or until softened. Add the bacon and continue to gently sauté for 5 to 8 minutes or until the bacon is crisp. Drain on paper towels.

Heat the wine in the fondue pan, then place over the lit burner. Toss the cheeses in the cornstarch then gradually stir into the wine, stirring continuously. Once the cheese has melted, stir in the drained bacon and shallots, paprika, chile sauce, and parsley. Heat until thick, then serve with the dippers, bread, and coleslaw.

Serves **8**
Preparation time **15 minutes**
Cooking time **20 to 23 minutes**

1 Tbsp butter
1 to 2 garlic cloves, peeled and crushed
4 shallots, peeled and chopped
8 oz smoked bacon strips, chopped
1 cup dry white wine
4 cups grated Gruyère cheese
2 cups grated Monterey Jack cheese
2 Tbsp cornstarch
1 tsp paprika
¼ to ½ tsp chile sauce, or to taste
1 Tbsp chopped fresh parsley

TO SERVE
Wedges of apple and fresh pineapple, celery and carrot sticks, cubes of crusty bread for dipping, and Zesty Orange Coleslaw *(see page 114).*

THANKSGIVING FONDUE

DON'T JUST KEEP THIS FONDUE FOR THE FALL–IT IS GOOD ENOUGH TO EAT ALL YEAR LONG.

Serves **6 to 8**
Preparation time **12 minutes**
Cooking time **12 to 14 minutes**

1 garlic clove
2/3 cup dry white wine
2/3 cup cranberry-apple juice
3 cups grated Emmentaler cheese
2 cups grated Monterey Jack cheese
2 Tbsp cornstarch
1 tsp dry mustard powder
2 Tbsp Calvados or other brandy

TO SERVE

Cubes of whole-wheat bread, strips of yellow and red bell pepper, carrot and celery sticks, apple wedges, broccoli florets, freshly cooked potatoes, Avocado & Mango Salad *(see page 106)*, and Chilled Ratatouille *(see page 109)*.

Cut the garlic and rub it on the insides of the fondue pot. Pour in the wine and cranberry and apple juice. Heat gently, then place over the lit burner.

Toss the cheeses in the cornstarch and mustard powder, then gradually stir into the wine. Cook, stirring continuously, until the cheese has melted.

Stir in the Calvados and continue to cook until thick and creamy. Serve with the dippers, potatoes, and salads.

BRANDY & WALNUT FONDUE

THE FLAVOR OF THE WALNUTS IS HEIGHTENED BY THE CALVADOS BRANDY AND CHEESE USED IN THIS FONDUE. IF CALVADOS IS UNAVAILABLE, ANY GOOD BRANDY CAN BE SUBSTITUTED.

Serves **6 to 8**
Preparation time **10 to 12 minutes**
Cooking time **10 minutes**

1 garlic clove
1 cup dry white wine
4 Tbsp Calvados brandy
2 cups grated mature Cheddar cheese
3 cups grated Gruyère cheese
1 cup crumbled goat cheese
2 Tbsp cornstarch
2 tsp Worcestershire sauce
1/2 tsp Tabasco Sauce, or to taste
1 cup chopped walnuts

TO SERVE

Cubes of crusty bread, strips of zucchini, apple and mango wedges, pickled jalapeño chiles for dipping, Chilled Ratatouille *(see page 109)*, and Tossed Green Salad *(see page 114)*.

Cut the garlic and rub it on the insides of the fondue pot. Pour in the wine and brandy. Heat gently, then place over the lit burner.

Toss the cheeses in the cornstarch then gradually stir into the wine. Heat gently, stirring until the cheese has melted.

Stir in the Worcestershire sauce, Tabasco Sauce, and walnuts. Continue to heat, stirring throughout until thick and creamy. Serve with the dippers and salads.

DUTCH CHEESE FONDUE

WITH A MILD CHEESE SUCH AS GOUDA, IT IS A GOOD IDEA TO ADD SOME MUSTARD AND CAYENNE PEPPER TO DEVELOP THE FLAVOR OF THE FONDUE.

Cut the garlic clove, then rub it on the insides of the fondue pot. Carefully place the pot over the lit burner. Pour in the wine and heat gently.

Gradually add the cheese, stirring throughout until the cheese has melted. Mix the mustard powder to a paste with the brandy and 1 tablespoon of water, then stir into the fondue. Add the cayenne pepper to taste.

Blend the cornstarch with 2 tablespoons of water and stir into the fondue. Cook for 2 to 3 minutes, stirring throughout until thickened, then serve with the bread and salad ingredients for dipping.

Serves **6**
Preparation time **10 minutes**
Cooking time **10 to 12 minutes**

1 garlic clove
1 cup dry white wine
1 lb grated Gouda cheese
1 to 2 tsp dry mustard powder
1 Tbsp brandy
Cayenne pepper
1½ Tbsp cornstarch

TO SERVE

Chunks of warm whole wheat bread, wedges of apple, cucumber, radishes, cherry tomatoes, and celery sticks for dipping.

RED BELL PEPPER & CHEESE FONDUE

I USUALLY PREFER TO SKIN BELL PEPPERS BEFORE USING AS THIS MAKES THEM MORE DIGESTIBLE (SEE CIDER & RED BELL PEPPER FONDUE, PAGE 84). HOWEVER, FOR DIPPERS, RAW PEPPERS ARE BETTER AS THEY STAY CRISP WHEN DIPPED INTO THE HOT FONDUE.

Pour the cider into the fondue pot and heat gently. Toss the Gruyère cheese in the cornstarch then slowly add to the cider, stirring well. When all the Gruyère has been added, stir in the Gorgonzola, bell pepper, corn, Tabasco Sauce, and pepper to taste. Continue to heat gently, still stirring, until the mixture becomes thick and creamy.

Stir the chopped basil, capers, and olives into the fondue pot and gently heat through.

Carefully place the fondue over the lit burner and serve with the dippers and salads.

Serves **6**
Preparation time **20 minutes including skinning the pepper**
Cooking time **10 minutes**

1 cup dry cider

3 cups grated Gruyère cheese

2 Tbsp cornstarch

1 cup crumbled Gorgonzola cheese

1 red bell pepper, seeded, skinned, and chopped

1¼ cups canned cream-style corn

¼ to ½ tsp Tabasco Sauce

Freshly ground black pepper

2 Tbsp chopped fresh basil

1 to 2 Tbsp capers

¼ cup pitted chopped black olives

TO SERVE

Cooked chipolata sausages, cubes of whole-wheat or focaccia bread, red and yellow bell pepper strips, celery, and carrot sticks for dipping. Spiced Rice Salad *(see page 109)* **and Mediterranean Salad** *(see page 112).*

MUSHROOM & ONION FONDUE

DRIED MUSHROOMS ARE READILY AVAILABLE IN MOST STORES. THEY ARE AN IDEAL INGREDIENT TO KEEP IN THE PANTRY AS THEY CAN QUICKLY BE REHYDRATED AND USED IN RISOTTOS, CASSEROLES, OMELETS, AND PASTA DISHES. WHEREVER POSSIBLE, USE THE SOAKING LIQUOR AS IT WILL BE FULL OF FLAVOR.

Cover the dried mushrooms with very hot (but not boiling) water and leave for 20 minutes. Drain, reserving ½ cup of the liquor, and chop fine the rehydrated mushrooms.

Heat the oil in the fondue pot and gently sauté the shallots, chile, and garlic for 5 minutes. Add the chopped button mushrooms and rehydrated mushrooms, and continue to sauté for 3 minutes. Sprinkle in the flour, cook for 2 more minutes, and gradually stir in the reserved soaking liquor, and then the wine and brandy. Carefully place over the lit burner.

Cook, stirring, until the mixture thickens, then gradually stir in the grated Gruyère. Continue to heat, stirring until the cheese has melted and the mixture is creamy.

Stir in the cream, heat gently, then serve with the dippers and salads.

Serves **6 to 8**
Preparation time **10 minutes**
  plus 20 minutes soaking time
Cooking time **20 minutes**

2 Tbsp dried mushrooms such as porcini or cèpes
3 Tbsp olive oil
4 shallots, chopped
1 red serrano chile, seeded and chopped
2 to 3 garlic cloves, crushed
1½ cups chopped closed-cap button mushrooms
3 Tbsp white all-purpose flour
1 cup dry white wine
2 Tbsp brandy
1 lb grated Gruyère cheese
2 Tbsp light cream

TO SERVE
Chunks of red and yellow bell pepper, zucchini sticks, cherry tomatoes, seedless red Tokay Flame and white grapes, cubes of focaccia bread for dipping. Chilled Ratatouille *(see page 109)*, **Tossed Green Salad** *(see page 114)*, **and Red Bean & Pepperoni Salad** *(see page 118)*.

SAGE FONDUE

IF YOU CANNOT FIND SAGE DERBY CHEESE, INCREASE THE AMOUNT OF GRUYÈRE, AND ADD SOME CHOPPED SAGE TO THE FONDUE.

Serves **4 to 6**
Preparation time **10 minutes**
Cooking time **10 minutes**

1 garlic clove
2 cups apple juice
3 cups grated Gruyère cheese
1 cup grated Sage Derby cheese
2 Tbsp cornstarch
1 to 2 Tbsp chopped fresh sage
Freshly ground black pepper

TO SERVE
Fresh apple and pear wedges, strips of red and yellow bell pepper, broccoli and cauliflower florets, and cherry tomatoes for dipping, Tossed Green Salad *(see page 114)*, and warm chunks of crusty whole wheat bread.

Cut the garlic and rub it on the insides of the fondue pot. Pour in the apple juice, and heat gently. Carefully place over the lit burner.

Toss the cheeses and cornstarch together, then gradually stir into the apple juice, stirring throughout until the cheese has melted.

Add the chopped sage and pepper to taste, then stir until thick and creamy. Serve with the dippers, Tossed Green Salad, and bread.

LAGER FONDUE

AS ITS NAME SUGGESTS, LAGER OR BEER WOULD BE THE IDEAL DRINK TO SERVE WITH THIS FONDUE.

Serves **4 to 6**
Preparation time **10 minutes**
Cooking time **10 to 12 minutes**

1 garlic clove
1 cup lager or light ale
2 cups grated Monterey Jack cheese
1 cup grated Emmentaler cheese
2 Tbsp cornstarch
1½ cups crumbled Roquefort cheese
¼ to ½ tsp Tabasco Sauce, or to taste
1 tsp Dijon mustard
Freshly ground black pepper

TO SERVE
Pickled jalapeño chiles, large pickled gherkins, large pitted olives, and cubes of warm French bread for dipping. Zesty Orange Coleslaw *(see page 114)*, Red Bean & Pepperoni Salad *(see page 118)*, and potato skins or wedges.

Cut the garlic and rub it on the inside of the fondue pot. Pour in the lager or light ale. Heat gently then carefully place the pot on the lit burner. Toss the Monterey Jack and Emmentaler cheeses in the cornstarch, then add to the pot. Cook gently, stirring well, until the cheese has melted.

Stir in the Roquefort, Tabasco Sauce, Dijon mustard, and freshly ground black pepper to taste. Continue to cook, stirring until the mixture is smooth and creamy. Serve with the dippers, salads, and potato skins or wedges.

MANHATTAN FONDUE

I AM PARTICULARLY FOND OF CREAM CHEESE THAT IS FLAVORED WITH BLACK PEPPER. HOWEVER, IF THIS IS NOT AVAILABLE, LOOK FOR CREAM CHEESE WITH OTHER FLAVORINGS, SUCH AS HERBS OR CHIVES. LOW-FAT CREAM CHEESE WORKS JUST AS WELL AS FULL-FAT.

Cut the garlic and rub it on the insides of the fondue pot, then pour in the wine. Heat gently, then carefully place over the lit burner.

Toss the Monterey Jack cheese in the cornstarch and gradually add to the wine, stirring throughout. Add the cream cheese and lemon juice. Continue to cook gently, stirring continuously until the mixture has thickened.

Stir in the chopped scallions, smoked salmon, and Tabasco Sauce to taste. Heat gently until thick, then serve with the dippers and salads.

Serves **4 to 6**
Preparation time **7 to 9 minutes**
Cooking time **10 minutes**

1 garlic clove
$^2/_3$ cup dry white wine
2$^1/_2$ cups grated Monterey Jack cheese
2 tsp cornstarch
$^3/_4$ cup cubed cream cheese with black pepper

1 Tbsp lemon juice
6 scallions, chopped
4 oz smoked salmon, chopped
Tabasco Sauce

TO SERVE
Pretzels, bread sticks, and cubed bagels for dipping. Sauerkraut Salad *(see page 107)* **and Artichoke Heart Salad** *(see page 115)*.

VIRGINIA FONDUE

MUSTARD HELPS TO BRING OUT THE FLAVOR OF THE CHEESE. IF WHOLE-GRAIN MUSTARD IS NOT AVAILABLE, ADD A TEASPOON OF DRIED MUSTARD POWDER TO THE FLOUR.

Melt the butter in the fondue pot and sprinkle in the flour. Cook for 2 minutes then stir in the mustard, horseradish, and then the milk. Continue to cook, stirring well until the mixture thickens.

Gradually stir in the grated cheeses, season to taste, then add the sherry.

Continue to cook until the mixture is thick and creamy. Stir in the chopped ham. Carefully transfer to the lit burner and serve with the dippers and salads.

Serves **4 to 6**
Preparation time **10 minutes**
Cooking time **12 to 14 minutes**

½ **stick butter**
3 **Tbsp white all-purpose flour**
1 **tsp whole-grain mustard**
1 **tsp creamed horseradish sauce**
1 **cup milk**
3 **cups grated Monterey Jack cheese**
1 **cup grated or crumbled feta cheese**
Salt and freshly ground black pepper
4 **Tbsp dry sherry**
6 **oz Virginia ham, chopped**

TO SERVE

Celery and carrot sticks, cauliflower florets, cherry tomatoes, button mushrooms, and cubes of rye bread for dipping. Sauerkraut Salad *(see page 107)***, Spicy Pepper & Mushroom Salad** *(see page 116)***, and Creamy Potato & Apple Salad** *(see page 117)***.**

VEGETABLES

CIDER & RED BELL PEPPER FONDUE

BELL PEPPERS TASTE BETTER AND ARE MORE DIGESTIBLE IF THEY ARE SKINNED BEFORE USING IN A COOKED DISH. SIMPLY CUT THE PEPPERS INTO QUARTERS AND PLACE UNDER A PREHEATED BROILER FOR ABOUT 10 MINUTES BEFORE PLACING IN A PLASTIC BAG UNTIL COOL, THEN SKINNING.

Melt the butter in the fondue pot and gently sauté the scallions for 3 minutes. Add the cider to the fondue pot. Heat through, then carefully place over the lit burner.

Add the grated cheese to the pot and heat, stirring until the cheese has melted.

Add the peppers, corn, and chopped olives, with black pepper to taste, and heat, stirring until thick and creamy. Just before serving, sprinkle in the chopped basil if using, garnish with the baby basil leaves, and serve with the dippers, sauce, and salads.

Serves **6**
Preparation time **10 to 12 minutes**
Cooking time **11 to 13 minutes**

1/2 stick butter
8 scallions, trimmed and chopped
1 1/4 cups medium-dry cider
4 cups grated Gruyère cheese
2 red bell peppers, skinned and chopped
3/4 cup canned corn kernels
1/2 cup pitted black or green olives, chopped
Freshly ground black pepper
1 Tbsp chopped fresh basil, optional

TO GARNISH
Baby basil leaves.

TO SERVE
Baby corn, bread sticks, pretzels, red, yellow, and green bell pepper strips, and fresh pear wedges for dipping. Green Tomatillo Sauce *(see page 100)*, **Artichoke Heart Salad** *(see page 115)*, **and Mint & Lemon Tabbouleh** *(see page 118)*.

APPLE & ARTICHOKE FONDUE

APPLE JUICE COMES BOTH FILTERED AND UNFILTERED. I WOULD RECOMMEND THE FILTERED VARIETY, NOT FOR TASTE BUT FOR APPEARANCE.

Heat the apple juice in the fondue pot and when hot place over the lit burner. Stir in the cheeses and continue to heat, stirring until the cheese has melted. Add the chopped artichoke hearts and scallions, then season with the pepper.

In a small bowl blend the cornstarch with the Calvados, and stir into the fondue. Continue to cook until thickened. Serve with the mayonnaise, dippers, and salads.

Serves **6 to 8**
Preparation time **10 minutes**
Cooking time **15 minutes**

1¼ cups apple juice
3 cups grated Emmentaler cheese
1 cup crumbled goat cheese
2 cups canned chopped artichoke hearts
6 scallions, chopped
Freshly ground black pepper
2 Tbsp cornstarch
3 Tbsp Calvados or other brandy

TO SERVE

Apple wedges, zucchini, carrot sticks, and crusty bread for dipping. Green Mayonnaise *(see page 96)*, Artichoke Heart Salad *(see page 115)*, and Spicy Pepper & Mushroom Salad *(see page 116)*.

APPLE & WATERCRESS FONDUE

SORREL WOULD MAKE AN EXCELLENT SUBSTITUTE FOR THE WATERCRESS.

Serves **4 to 6**
Preparation time **10 minutes**
Cooking time **15 minutes**

1 garlic clove
1 cup apple juice
2 Tbsp brandy
2½ cups grated Emmentaler cheese
1 cup crumbled Gorgonzola cheese
1 Tbsp cornstarch
2 tsp liquid honey
Freshly ground black pepper
½ cup chopped watercress

TO SERVE
Watercress sprigs, wedges of apple and pineapple, blanched asparagus spears, pickled onions, and cubes of soda or whole-wheat bread for dipping. Mint & Lemon Tabbouleh (*see page 118*).

Cut the garlic and rub it on the insides of the fondue pot. Pour in the apple juice and brandy. Carefully place over the lit burner and heat gently.

Toss the cheeses in the cornstarch then gradually add them to the apple juice, stirring continuously.

When all the cheese has been added, stir in the honey and add pepper to taste. Cook, stirring until thick and creamy.

Stir the chopped watercress into the fondue and serve with the dippers and salad.

AVOCADO & PECAN FONDUE

LOOK FOR AVOCADOS THAT ARE RIPE, BUT NOT REALLY SOFT OTHERWISE THE COLOR OF THE FONDUE WILL NOT BE GOOD.

Serves **4 to 6**
Preparation time **12 to 15 minutes**
Cooking time **15 minutes**

6 scallions, chopped
1 cup dry white wine
2 large ripe avocados
2 Tbsp lemon juice
2½ cups grated Gruyère cheese
1 cup crumbled blue cheese, such as Gorgonzola
1 Tbsp cornstarch
½ cup chopped pecans
3 Tbsp light cream
Freshly grated nutmeg

TO SERVE
Bread sticks, pretzels, cooked jumbo shrimp, melon, and fresh pear wedges for dipping. Artichoke & Bean Salad with Vinaigrette (*see page 110*), Tossed Green Salad (*see page 114*), and freshly cooked potato skins.

Gently sauté the scallions in the wine for 3 minutes.

Peel and halve the avocados, and discard the pits. Mash the flesh with the lemon juice and reserve.

Toss the cheeses in the cornstarch, then slowly stir into the fondue pot. Cook, stirring, until the cheeses have melted.

Stir the mashed avocado into the fondue, then stir in the pecans and cream. Add nutmeg to taste. Cook, stirring until thickened. Serve with the dippers, salads, and potato skins.

ASIAN VEGETABLE FONDUE

IT IS POSSIBLE TO BUY READY-PREPARED *DIM SUM* SNACKS, WHICH WOULD BE IDEAL TO SERVE AS DIPPERS FOR THIS FONDUE. ADDING A LITTLE SESAME OIL TO THE COOKING OIL WILL HELP TO GIVE AN ASIAN FLAVOR.

Prepare the vegetables, cutting them into thin strips or chunks where necessary. If you prefer a softer vegetable after cooking, dip in boiling water for 3 to 5 minutes, drain, and arrange in small bowls. Cut the tofu into cubes and arrange in small bowls.

Using a whisk, blend the egg yolk with the water, flour, and 1 teaspoon of the sesame oil until smooth. Whisk the egg white until stiff, then stir into the batter, cover, and leave for 30 minutes.

Heat the oil and the remaining sesame oil in a Mongolian hot pot or fondue pot and carefully place over the lit burner.

Spear the vegetables and tofu cubes onto the fondue forks and dip into the prepared batter, then into the hot oil. Cook for 2 to 3 minutes or until golden. Spear the *dim sum* onto the fondue forks and without first dipping into the batter, cook in the hot oil.

Garnish with the chopped scallions and serve with the dipping sauces, salad, and rice.

Serves **6**

Preparation time **15 minutes plus 30 minutes standing time for the batter**

Cooking time **2 to 3 minutes per vegetable**

1 cup baby corn

1 cup small asparagus spears

1½ cups water chestnuts

1 red bell pepper, seeded

1 yellow bell pepper, seeded

2 cups bamboo shoots

1½ cups firm tofu

1 medium egg, separated

⅔ cup ice-cold water

1 cup white all-purpose flour

3 tsp sesame oil

1 pt oil, for frying

1 packet prepared *dim sum*, optional

TO GARNISH

Chopped scallions.

TO SERVE

Soy sauce, *hoisin* **sauce, Sweet & Sour Sauce** *(see page 97)*, **Mixed Chinese Green Salad** *(see page 108)*, **and freshly cooked glutinous (short-grain) rice.**

SPINACH FONDUE

FRESH SPINACH IS READILY AVAILABLE IN MOST FRESH PRODUCE MARKETS. HOWEVER, USING THE FROZEN VARIETY SAVES TIME AS IT IS ALREADY WASHED AND CHOPPED. IF USING FROZEN SPINACH WITH THIS FONDUE, FIRST THAW IT AND SQUEEZE OUT ANY EXCESS MOISTURE.

Melt the butter in the fondue pot and gently sauté the onion and garlic for 5 minutes, or until softened. Add the cider and heat through, then carefully place over the lit burner.

Toss the cheeses in the cornstarch then stir into the fondue pot. Squeeze any excess moisture from the spinach and chop fine. Add to the fondue pot and cook until the mixture is smooth and creamy.

Stir in the lemon zest, juice, honey, and black pepper to taste, and continue to heat for 5 minutes before serving with the dippers and salads.

Serves **5 to 6**
Preparation time **15 minutes**
Cooking time **12 to 15 minutes**

½ **stick butter**

1 **medium onion, chopped fine**

2 to 3 **garlic cloves, crushed**

1¼ **cups dry cider**

2 **cups grated Emmentaler cheese**

1 **cup crumbled Gorgonzola cheese**

2 **Tbsp cornstarch**

1 **cup thawed frozen spinach**

1 **Tbsp grated lemon zest**

2 to 3 **Tbsp lemon juice**

1 to 2 **tsp liquid honey or to taste**

Freshly ground black pepper

TO SERVE

Bread sticks, celery and apple wedges, cubes of salami, and chipolata sausages, for dipping. Artichoke & Bean Salad with Vinaigrette *(see page 113)* **and Zesty Orange Coleslaw** *(see page 114).*

ONION & CARAWAY FONDUE

LOOK FOR THE DIFFERENT VARIETIES OF ONIONS THAT ARE NOW AVAILABLE. I LIKE WHITE ONIONS AS THEY ARE SWEETER THAN YELLOW ONIONS.

Serves **4**
Preparation time **10 minutes**
Cooking time **20 minutes**

1/2 stick butter
1 lb onions, chopped
2 to 3 garlic cloves, peeled and crushed
1 to 2 tsp caraway seeds
2/3 cup dry white wine
2 1/2 cups grated Gruyère cheese
1 cup crumbled feta cheese
2 Tbsp cornstarch

1 tsp whole-grain mustard
Freshly ground black pepper
1/4 tsp grated nutmeg

TO SERVE
Frankfurter sausages, pepperoni sticks, cubes of pumpernickel bread, and pretzels, for dipping. Sauerkraut Salad *(see page 107)*, Tossed Green Salad *(see page 114)*, and Creamy Potato & Apple Salad *(see page 117)*.

Melt the butter in the fondue pot, then gently sauté the onions and garlic for 10 to 15 minutes or until softened. Stir in the caraway seeds and cook for 2 minutes. Add the wine and heat through, then place over the lit burner.

Toss the cheeses in the cornstarch then gradually stir into the fondue pot and continue stirring until all the cheese has melted.

Stir in the mustard, add pepper to taste, and add the nutmeg. Heat through gently until the mixture is thick and creamy. Serve with the dippers and salads.

ASPARAGUS FONDUE

THIS FONDUE IS VERY QUICK TO MAKE, AND IS IDEAL TO SERVE WHEN FRIENDS VISIT UNEXPECTEDLY.

Serves **4**
Preparation time **10 minutes**
Cooking time **15 minutes**

2 to 3 garlic cloves, crushed
6 to 8 fresh asparagus spears, chopped
1 1/4 cups apple juice
2 Tbsp medium-dry sherry
3 cups grated Emmentaler cheese
2 Tbsp cornstarch
Tabasco Sauce, to taste
Freshly ground black pepper

TO SERVE
Fresh blanched asparagus spears, cucumber and carrot sticks, and artichoke hearts for dipping. Freshly cooked new potatoes and Tossed Green Salad *(see page 114)*.

In a pan, gently sauté the garlic and asparagus in the apple juice for 5 minutes, or until softened. Add the sherry. Stir gently until well blended and hot, then pour into the fondue pot and carefully place over the lit burner.

Toss the cheese in the cornstarch then stir into the pot and cook, stirring until the cheese has melted. Season to taste with the Tabasco Sauce and black pepper, and cook until thick and creamy. Serve with the dippers, potatoes, and salad.

MIXED VEGETABLE FONDUE

WHEN CHOOSING THE VEGETABLES FOR THIS FONDUE, SELECT A GOOD VARIETY OF COLORS, SHAPES, AND TEXTURES, TO MAKE AN ATTRACTIVE AND APPEALING MEAL.

Using a whisk, blend the egg yolk with the water, apple juice, flour, and olive oil until smooth. Whisk the egg white until stiff. Stir into the batter, cover, and stand for at least 30 minutes.

Prepare the vegetables, dividing the cauliflower and broccoli into small florets. Blanch in boiling water for 2 minutes, drain, and refresh in cold water, then drain thoroughly and pat dry with paper towels. Wash and pat the pepper strips dry. Rinse and dry the zucchini strips. Dip the carrot strips in boiling water for 2 minutes, then drain and pat dry. Wash the artichoke hearts and pat dry with paper towels. Wipe the mushrooms well.

Heat the oil in the fondue pot, then carefully place over the lit burner.

Dip the prepared vegetables into the batter, and spear onto fondue forks. Cook in the hot oil for 2 to 3 minutes or until golden. Serve with the dipping sauces, salad, and potatoes.

Serves **6**
Preparation time **15 minutes plus 30 minutes standing time for batter**
Cooking time **2 to 3 minutes per vegetable**

1 small egg, separated
¾ cup ice-cold water
¼ cup apple juice
1 cup white all-purpose flour
1 tsp olive oil
1½ lbs assorted vegetables, such as cauliflower and broccoli florets, strips of assorted bell peppers, zucchini and carrot sticks, artichoke hearts, and mushrooms
1 pt oil, for frying

TO SERVE
Blue Cheese Dressing *(see page 96)*, **Salsa** *(see page 99)*, **Madeira Sauce** *(see page 103)*, **Spiced Rice Salad** *(see page 109)*, **and freshly cooked new potatoes.**

GUACAMOLE FONDUE

AVOCADOS HAVE A WONDERFUL CREAMY TEXTURE AND A NUTTY FLAVOR. TO PREVENT THE FONDUE FROM DISCOLORING, PREPARE IT AT THE VERY LAST MOMENT AND MIX WITH LEMON OR LIME JUICE.

Cut the garlic and rub it on the insides of the fondue pot, then pour in the white wine. Carefully place over the lit burner and heat gently. Toss the cheeses in the cornstarch, then gradually stir them into the wine. Heat gently, stirring throughout until the cheese has melted, then stir in the tomato paste.

Peel and pit the avocado and mash well, pour over the lemon or lime juice, and mix lightly. Stir into the cheese mixture with the sour cream. Add black pepper to taste. Heat gently, stirring until the mixture is thick and creamy. Serve with the dippers, dipping sauces, and salad.

Serves **4 to 6**
Preparation time **10 to 15 minutes**
Cooking time **10 minutes**

1 garlic clove
⅔ cup dry white wine
3 cups grated Gruyère cheese
1 cup crumbled feta cheese
2 Tbsp cornstarch
2 Tbsp tomato paste
1 large avocado
3 Tbsp lemon or lime juice
3 Tbsp sour cream
Freshly ground black pepper

TO SERVE
Avocado wedges, tossed in lemon juice, pickled jalapeño chiles, red bell pepper strips, and strips of warm pita bread for dipping. Salsa *(see page 99)*, **Sour Cream Sauce** *(see page 103)*, **and Tossed Green Salad** *(see page 114)*.

SAUCES & DIPS

BLUE CHEESE DRESSING

I HAVE USED ROQUEFORT CHEESE IN THIS RECIPE, BUT YOU CAN USE ANY BLUE CHEESE. LOOK FOR A CREAMY CHEESE THAT WILL BREAK DOWN EASILY AND COMBINE WELL WITH THE OTHER INGREDIENTS.

Makes **1½ cups**
Preparation time
  5 minutes
Chilling time
  30 minutes

- 1 cup sour cream
- 3 Tbsp low-fat plain yogurt
- ¾ cup Roquefort cheese
- 2 Tbsp lemon juice
- 2 tsp brandy, optional
- 2 Tbsp chopped fresh chives
- Salt and freshly ground black pepper

Place the sour cream in a bowl and stir in the yogurt. Crumble the cheese, then stir into the sour cream mixture.

Add the remaining ingredients, then turn into a serving bowl, cover, and chill in the refrigerator for 30 minutes before serving.

GREEN MAYONNAISE

ALTHOUGH SOME COMMERCIALLY MADE MAYONNAISE IS GOOD, NOTHING COMPARES WITH THE GENUINE ARTICLE. IF YOU DO NOT HAVE A FOOD PROCESSOR, YOU CAN BEAT THE INGREDIENTS BY HAND.

Makes **1 cup**
Preparation time
  5 to 6 minutes

- 1 egg yolk
- ½ tsp salt
- ½ tsp dry mustard powder
- Freshly ground black pepper
- ½ tsp superfine sugar
- ⅔ cup olive oil
- 1 to 2 Tbsp lemon juice
- 2 shallots, peeled and chopped fine
- 4 Tbsp chopped fresh watercress
- 1 Tbsp chopped fresh parsley
- 2 Tbsp chopped toasted pine nuts

Place the egg yolk with the seasonings and sugar in the bowl of the food processor and switch on. Keeping the speed low, gradually add the oil, a little at a time.

Once all the oil has been added, slowly add the lemon juice.

Stir in the chopped shallots, watercress, parsley, and pine nuts. Turn into a serving bowl, cover, and store in the refrigerator until required. Stir before using.

SWEET & SOUR SAUCE

THE TANG IN THIS SAUCE IS ESPECIALLY GOOD WITH RICH FOODS SUCH AS PORK AND OILY FISH. IT IS ALSO GOOD WITH CHICKEN AND TURKEY DISHES.

Heat the oil in a pan and gently sauté the pepper and scallions for 3 minutes.

Add the chicken broth, soy sauce, vinegar, ginger, and honey, then simmer for 3 minutes. Bring to a boil.

Blend the cornstarch with the pineapple juice, stir into the sauce, and cook, stirring until the sauce thickens. Serve.

Makes **2 cups**
Preparation time **5 to 7 minutes**
Cooking time **8 to 10 minutes**

1 Tbsp oil
1 red bell pepper, seeded and chopped
6 scallions, trimmed and chopped
²⁄₃ cup chicken broth
1 Tbsp dark soy sauce
1 Tbsp red wine vinegar
2 Tbsp chopped preserved ginger
1 to 2 tsp liquid honey
2 Tbsp cornstarch
¹⁄₃ cup pineapple juice

QUICK SATAY SAUCE

A SPEEDY ALTERNATIVE TO THE REGULAR SATAY SAUCE, THIS VERSION IS MADE IN A MATTER OF MINUTES.

Blend all the ingredients, except the coconut milk, until smooth. Slowly stir in the coconut milk, then pour into a pan and heat gently.

Cook gently for about 2 to 4 minutes or until heated. Serve warm or cold, according to preference.

Makes **1¼ cups**
Preparation time **3 to 4 minutes**
Cooking time **2 to 4 minutes**

6 Tbsp smooth or chunky peanut butter
½ tsp hot chili powder
½ tsp ground ginger
2 Tbsp lemon juice
1 Tbsp dark soy sauce
⅔ cup coconut milk

SATAY SAUCE

THIS IS RAPIDLY BECOMING A VERY POPULAR
SAUCE AND CAN BE USED AS A SAUCE OR
DIP, AS WELL AS A MARINADE FOR FISH, POULTRY,
MEATS, OR VEGETABLE CRUDITÉS.

Makes **2 cups**
Preparation time
8 minutes
Cooking time
10 to 11 minutes

2 Tbsp oil

2 medium onions, chopped or grated

2 to 3 garlic cloves, crushed

$\frac{1}{2}$ to 1 tsp hot chili powder

$\frac{1}{2}$ cup roasted peanuts

$\frac{2}{3}$ cup warm water

1 Tbsp granulated brown sugar

1 Tbsp lemon juice

1 Tbsp dark soy sauce

Heat the oil, then add one of the onions and fry for 5 minutes
or until soft.

Place the remaining onion with the garlic, chili powder,
and peanuts in a food processor and blend to form a paste.

Gradually stir the paste into the cooked onion and cook for
2 to 3 minutes. Slowly stir in the water, then add the sugar,
lemon juice, and soy sauce. Bring to a boil and boil gently for
2 minutes or until a chunky sauce is formed. Serve.

SALSA

ADD FRESH FRUITS, VEGETABLES, AND SPICES
TO THE BASIC RECIPE BELOW FOR DIFFERENT
SALSA COMBINATIONS.

Makes **1 cup**
Preparation time
6 to 8 minutes
Chilling time
30 minutes

1$\frac{1}{2}$ cups ripe tomatoes, peeled and seeded

1 to 2 jalapeño chiles, seeded and chopped

4 scallions, chopped

1 to 2 tsp warmed liquid honey

2 Tbsp chopped fresh cilantro

Salt and freshly ground black pepper

2-inch piece cucumber, skinned and seeded

Finely chop the tomatoes and place in a bowl with the chiles,
scallions, honey, and cilantro. Season to taste.

Finely chop the cucumber and stir into the salsa. Spoon into a
serving bowl, cover, and chill for 30 minutes.

VARIATIONS
Add a small, ripe, peeled and chopped mango to the basic salsa
and stir in a tablespoon of toasted sesame seeds.

Toss a ripe, peeled and diced avocado in 2 tablespoons of lemon
juice and stir into the basic salsa recipe.

Substitute 1$\frac{1}{2}$ cups of peeled, seeded, and chopped green
tomatillos for the ripe tomatoes; then cook gently in 2 tablespoons
of white wine. Add to the basic salsa with 2 tablespoons of raisins.

TARTAR SAUCE

TARTAR SAUCE COMBINES WELL WITH ALL KINDS OF FISH, VEGETABLES, AND SOME POULTRY DISHES. IT CAN BE MADE AHEAD OF TIME, THEN STORED FOR UP TO TWO DAYS IF COVERED AND KEPT IN THE REFRIGERATOR.

Makes **1 cup**
Preparation time
6 to 8 minutes

1 egg yolk
½ tsp dry mustard
½ tsp salt
Freshly ground black pepper
½ tsp superfine sugar
⅔ cup olive oil
1 Tbsp white wine vinegar
2 tsp chopped fresh tarragon
2 tsp chopped fresh parsley
1 Tbsp chopped capers
1 Tbsp chopped gherkins
1 to 2 Tbsp lemon juice

Place the egg yolk in a bowl with the mustard, salt, black pepper to taste, and sugar. Mix well, then very slowly add the oil, drop by drop, all the time whisking well. Continue to whisk until a thick and smooth sauce is formed.

When all the oil has been added, stir in the white wine vinegar, chopped herbs, capers, gherkins, and lemon juice. Stir until blended, then spoon into a bowl, cover, and leave for about 1 hour to allow the flavors to develop. Serve.

GREEN TOMATILLO SAUCE

TOMATILLOS ARE A VARIETY OF GREEN TOMATO WITH INFLATED PAPERY SKINS. THEY HAVE A BITTER FLAVOR WITH OVERTONES OF LEMON. THE BITTERNESS IS LOST WHEN THE FRUIT IS COOKED. CANNED TOMATILLOS CAN BE BOUGHT IN SPECIALTY FOOD STORES. YOU CAN SUBSTITUTE GREEN TOMATOES IF TOMATILLOS ARE NOT AVAILABLE, BUT ADD A LITTLE LEMON JUICE TO RECREATE THE LEMONY FLAVOR.

Makes **1¼ cups**
Preparation time
8 minutes
Cooking time
15 minutes

1 Tbsp oil
1 to 2 garlic cloves, crushed
1 to 2 red serrano chiles, chopped
  and seeded
1⅔ cups tomatillos, chopped
⅔ cup vegetable broth
1 to 2 tsp liquid honey
Salt and freshly ground black pepper
2 Tbsp chopped fresh cilantro
2 Tbsp lime juice
1 to 1½ Tbsp arrowroot

Heat the oil in a pan and gently sauté the garlic, chiles, and tomatillos for 5 minutes. Add the broth and honey, season to taste, then simmer for 10 minutes or until the tomatillos are soft and pulpy.

Rub through a fine-meshed strainer and return to the cleaned pan. Add the cilantro, blend the lime juice and arrowroot together, and stir into the pan. Cook, stirring, until the sauce thickens and clears. Adjust the seasoning and serve warm or cold.

TOMATO DEVILED SAUCE

THERE ARE MANY READY-PREPARED MUSTARDS NOW COMMERCIALLY AVAILABLE. HOWEVER, FOR DEPTH OF FLAVOR AND GREATER CONTROL, I PREFER TO USE MUSTARD POWDER AS IT ONLY BECOMES FIERCE WHEN MIXED TO A PASTE WITH WATER.

Melt the butter in a pan and gently sauté the onion, chile, and garlic for 3 minutes. Add the chopped bell pepper with the mustard powder and flour, and cook for a further 2 minutes.

Add the tomatoes, then blend the tomato paste with the broth or water, and add to the pan with the Worcestershire sauce. Bring to a boil, then cover and simmer for 10 minutes, stirring occasionally.

Add the seasoning to taste, stir well, and serve the sauce hot.

Makes **1½ cups**
Preparation time **6 to 8 minutes**
Cooking time **15 minutes**

1 Tbsp butter

1 small onion, chopped

1 red serrano chile, seeded and chopped

1 to 2 garlic cloves, crushed

1 small red bell pepper, seeded and chopped

1 to 3 tsp dry mustard powder

1 Tbsp white all-purpose flour

1½ cups tomatoes, peeled and chopped

1 Tbsp tomato paste

4 Tbsp broth or water

1 to 2 tsp Worcestershire sauce

Salt and freshly ground black pepper

ORANGE CUMBERLAND
DIPPING SAUCE

USE A ZESTER IF YOU HAVE ONE TO REMOVE THE ZEST FROM THE ORANGE AND LEMON.
IF NOT, REMOVE AS FINE A LAYER OF PEEL AS POSSIBLE AND CUT INTO VERY THIN STRIPS.
BLANCH FOR A LITTLE LONGER.

Remove the zest from the orange and lemon, slice fine, and blanch in boiling water for 1 to 3 minutes (depending on thickness). Remove and refresh in cold water. Drain and reserve.

Squeeze the juice from the fruits and strain into a pan. Add the marmalade, red wine, sugar, and seasoning to taste.

Bring to a boil. Blend the arrowroot with 1 tablespoon of water, then stir into the pan. Cook, stirring until the sauce thickens and clears. Stir in the reserved blanched fruit zest and serve.

Makes **1 cup**
Preparation time **5 minutes**
Cooking time **5 minutes**

1 orange

1 lemon

6 Tbsp orange marmalade

4 Tbsp red wine

2 Tbsp granulated light brown sugar

Salt and freshly ground black pepper

1 tsp arrowroot

MADEIRA SAUCE

WHENEVER I OPEN A BOTTLE OF MADEIRA OR PORT,
I ALWAYS TRY TO FIND A WAY OF USING IT UP FAIRLY
QUICKLY, AS THESE DRINKS DO NOT LAST LONG ONCE
OPENED. A GOOD WAY TO DO THIS IS BY MAKING THE
FOLLOWING SAUCE, WHICH HAS NOW BECOME A
FAVORITE OF MINE.

Makes **1¼ cups**
Preparation time
  5 minutes
Cooking time
  10 minutes

- 1 Tbsp butter
- ½ cup chopped fine mushrooms
- 1 cup chopped tomatoes, peeled and seeded
- 1 Tbsp white all-purpose flour
- ⅔ cup Madeira
- 2 Tbsp orange juice
- 1 Tbsp liquid honey
- Salt and freshly ground black pepper

Melt the butter in a pan and gently sauté the mushrooms for 5 minutes. Add the tomatoes and continue to cook for 2 minutes.

Sprinkle in the flour and cook for 2 minutes, then take the pan off the heat and gradually stir in the Madeira before adding the orange juice.

Return to the heat and cook, stirring, until the sauce thickens. Stir in the honey with seasoning to taste.

Simmer for 2 minutes, and serve.

SOUR CREAM SAUCE

THIS SAUCE IS IDEAL SERVED WITH STEAKS
AND LAMB DISHES. FOR A HEALTHIER VERSION
SUBSTITUTE LOW-FAT PLAIN OR GREEK YOGURT
FOR HALF THE SOUR CREAM. SHERRY, WHITE WINE,
OR RASPBERRY VINEGAR CAN BE USED IN PLACE
OF THE TARRAGON VINEGAR.

Makes **1 cup**
Preparation time
  5 minutes plus
  30 minutes
  marinating time

- ⅔ cup sour cream
- 1 small onion, chopped fine
- 1 Tbsp chopped capers
- ¼ tsp salt
- ½ tsp freshly ground black pepper
- 1 Tbsp chopped fresh parsley
- 2 Tbsp tarragon vinegar

Place the sour cream into a bowl, then stir in the onion, capers, salt, and pepper. Add the parsley, then slowly stir in the vinegar until well blended.

Turn into a serving bowl, cover, and leave in the refrigerator for at least 30 minutes to allow the flavors to develop.

INDIAN-STYLE RAITA

THIS SAUCE IS SMOOTH, CREAMY, AND VERY COOL ON THE PALATE. IT IS IDEAL SERVED WITH HOT, SPICY DISHES OR WHEN THE WEATHER IS REALLY HOT.

Makes **1 1/2 cups**
Preparation time
5 minutes
Chilling time
30 minutes

1 1/4 cups low-fat plain yogurt
3-inch piece of cucumber
2 Tbsp chopped fresh cilantro
1 Tbsp chopped fresh parsley
1 Tbsp grated lime zest
Salt and freshly ground black pepper

Place the yogurt into a small bowl. Thinly peel the cucumber and discard the seeds. Dice fine.

Add the cucumber to the yogurt and stir in the chopped herbs, lime zest, and seasoning to taste. Lightly mix together.

Spoon into a serving bowl and cover lightly. Chill in the refrigerator for 30 minutes before serving.

CREAMY HERB MAYONNAISE

VARY THE HERBS ACCORDING TO THE FOOD BEING SERVED. DIFFERENT HERBS MARRY WELL WITH DIFFERENT FOODS (SEE BELOW).

Makes **1 cup**
Preparation time
8 to 9 minutes

2 egg yolks
1/2 tsp whole-grain mustard
1/2 tsp salt
1/2 tsp freshly ground black pepper
1/2 tsp superfine sugar
2/3 cup olive oil
2 Tbsp lemon juice
2 Tbsp chopped fresh herbs (see below)
1 egg white

Beat the egg yolks with the mustard, seasonings, and sugar, then add the oil drop by drop, beating vigorously until the mayonnaise is smooth and creamy.

Stir in the lemon juice with the chopped fresh herbs, cover, and leave in the refrigerator until required. Just before serving, whisk the egg white until stiff, stir into the mayonnaise, and serve.

Try dill, tarragon, parsley, and chives with fish. With poultry use a few of the following: chervil, parsley, cilantro, tarragon, basil, and sage. With steak use sage, thyme, oregano, and rosemary. With pork, use a few of the following: sage, thyme, oregano, parsley, and cilantro. Lamb goes well with rosemary, basil, oregano, marjoram, and cilantro.

SALADS

AVOCADO & MANGO SALAD

MANY FONDUES ARE QUITE RICH AND A FRESH, CRISP SALAD MAKES AN IDEAL ACCOMPANIMENT. THIS SALAD, WITH
ITS BITTER SALAD LEAVES, IS WONDERFUL SERVED WITH RICH CHEESE FONDUES.

Serves **4**
Preparation time **8 to 10 minutes**

1 large, ripe avocado

2 Tbsp lime juice

1 large, ripe mango

1 cup bitter salad leaves such as radicchio,
   arugula, baby spinach leaves, frisée

6 scallions, trimmed and chopped

1 cup quartered cherry tomatoes

¼ cup toasted pine nuts

DRESSING

3 Tbsp olive oil

1 Tbsp walnut oil

2 Tbsp orange juice

Salt and freshly ground black pepper

1 tsp whole-grain mustard

1 to 2 tsp liquid honey

Peel and pit the avocado, then slice, and toss in the lime juice. Peel the mango and slice thinly.

Rinse the salad leaves, shake off the excess water, and place in a salad bowl. Arrange the sliced avocado, mango, scallions, and tomatoes on top, then toss lightly together. Sprinkle over the toasted pine nuts. Place all the ingredients for the dressing together in a screw-top jar and shake vigorously. Pour over the salad and serve.

SAUERKRAUT SALAD

IF YOU FIND SAUERKRAUT IS USUALLY TOO SHARP FOR YOUR PALATE, ADD A LITTLE EXTRA HONEY TO THE DRESSING—YOU WILL BE PLEASANTLY SURPRISED AT THE DIFFERENCE THIS WILL MAKE.

Serves **6**
Preparation time
   5 to 8 minutes

2 cups prepared sauerkraut,
   fresh or canned

1 medium onion, chopped fine

4 large gherkins

2 red dessert apples

2 Tbsp lemon juice

1 Tbsp chopped fresh parsley

1 Tbsp chopped fresh basil

DRESSING

5 Tbsp olive oil

2 Tbsp lemon juice

2 to 3 tsp liquid honey

Salt and freshly ground
   black pepper

1 tsp caraway seeds

Drain the sauerkraut, rinse thoroughly, and dry well on paper towels. Place in a bowl with the chopped onion.

Finely chop the gherkins and add to the bowl. Wash, core, and chop the apples and toss in the lemon juice, then add to the bowl with the chopped herbs.

Place all the ingredients for the dressing in a screw-top jar and shake vigorously, then pour over the salad and serve.

MIXED CHINESE GREEN SALAD

AS WITH MOST SALADS, THIS IS BEST MADE JUST BEFORE IT IS REQUIRED. TOSS IN THE DRESSING AND THEN SERVE.

Place the bok choy in a large bowl with the scallions. Thinly peel the cucumber and cut into half-moon shapes, and add to the bok choy with the celery, bell pepper, and bean sprouts.

Make the dressing by placing all the ingredients in a screw-top jar. Shake vigorously until well blended.

Just before serving, toss the salad in the prepared dressing, place in a serving bowl, and sprinkle with the chopped cilantro and peanuts.

Serves **6**
Preparation time **5 to 6 minutes**

2 cups rinsed and finely shredded bok choy
8 scallions, trimmed and chopped
½ small cucumber
4 celery stalks, trimmed and chopped
1 green bell pepper, seeded and sliced
2 cups bean sprouts
2 Tbsp chopped fresh cilantro
2 Tbsp unsalted roasted peanuts,
  roughly chopped

DRESSING
4 Tbsp oil
1 tsp sesame oil
1 Tbsp dark soy sauce
2 Tbsp orange juice
Salt and freshly ground
  black pepper

CHILLED RATATOUILLE

IF YOU ARE PLANNING AN INFORMAL FONDUE, WITH FRIENDS SITTING IN THE LIVING ROOM OR OUTSIDE, IT WILL BE EASIER TO EAT SALADS THAT ARE CUT INTO BITE-SIZE PIECES.

Serves **4 to 6**
Preparation time
  12 to 15 minutes plus
  30 minutes chilling time
Cooking time **20 minutes**

4 Tbsp olive oil
1 medium onion, peeled and sliced
2 to 3 garlic cloves, crushed
1 medium eggplant, cubed
1 red bell pepper, seeded and sliced
1 yellow bell pepper, seeded
  and sliced
1 zucchini, sliced
1½ cups chopped tomatoes
1 cup sliced mushrooms
3 Tbsp white wine
Salt and freshly ground black pepper
2 Tbsp chopped fresh basil

Heat the oil in a large pan and sauté the onion, garlic, and eggplant for 5 minutes. Add the bell peppers, zucchini, tomatoes, mushrooms, and white wine, cover with a lid, and cook gently for 10 minutes, stirring occasionally.

Season to taste, and continue to cook gently for 5 minutes or until the vegetables are tender but still retaining their shape.

Cool, chill for at least 30 minutes, and serve sprinkled with the chopped basil.

SPICED RICE SALAD

CHOOSE YOUR FAVORITE KIND OF RICE FOR THIS SALAD. A MIXTURE OF WHITE RICE AND WILD, OR THAI RICE GO PARTICULARLY WELL.

Serves **6**
Preparation time **10 minutes**
Cooking time **15 to 18 minutes**

1 cup rice (see above)
1 tsp ground cumin
½ tsp ground coriander
2 large carrots, peeled and grated
8 scallions, trimmed and chopped
1 red bell pepper, seeded
  and chopped
¾ cup raisins
2 Tbsp chopped fresh cilantro

DRESSING
4 Tbsp olive oil
2 Tbsp orange juice
½ tsp ground coriander
½ to 1 tsp crushed chiles
Salt and freshly ground
  black pepper

Cook the rice in lightly salted boiling water for 15 to 18 minutes, or until cooked. Drain and place in a bowl. Add the ground cumin and coriander.

Stir in the carrots, scallions, bell pepper, raisins, and chopped cilantro. Lightly toss together.

Place all the ingredients for the dressing in a screw-top jar and shake vigorously, then pour over the salad, and serve.

ARTICHOKE & BEAN SALAD WITH
VINAIGRETTE

USE EITHER ARTICHOKE HEARTS OR BOTTOMS FOR THIS BEAN SALAD. WHICHEVER YOU USE, THE RESULT
WILL BE DELICIOUS.

Trim the beans, cut into short lengths, and cook in lightly salted boiling water for 5 to 7 minutes or until tender but still retaining some crispness. Drain and refresh in cold water. Drain and place in a bowl.

Drain all the canned beans and rinse, then add to the French beans with the artichoke hearts or bottoms, olives, and scallions.

Blend the dressing ingredients, pour over the salad, stir lightly, and serve.

Serves **6**
Preparation time **8 to 10 minutes**
Cooking time **5 to 7 minutes**

2 cups French beans
2 cups canned cannellini beans
1 cup canned red kidney beans
2 cups canned artichoke hearts
  or bottoms
½ cup green and black olives, pitted
6 scallions, trimmed and chopped

DRESSING
6 Tbsp olive oil
2 Tbsp white wine vinegar
1 tsp superfine sugar
Salt and freshly ground
  black pepper
1 Tbsp chopped fresh parsley
1 Tbsp chopped fresh cilantro

TO GARNISH
Fresh cilantro sprigs.

MEDITERRANEAN SALAD

IF YOU ARE LUCKY ENOUGH TO LIVE NEAR A GOOD DELI, LOOK FOR LARGE, PLUMP, MARINATED OLIVES FOR THIS SALAD. THERE ARE MANY VARIETIES AVAILABLE—ALL DELICIOUS—THE ONLY PROBLEM IS THAT YOU WILL NEED TO BUY DOUBLE THE AMOUNT CALLED FOR, TO ALLOW FOR INEVITABLE SNACKING!

Place the artichoke hearts in a bowl. Rinse the tomatoes and halve, then add to the bowl.

Wipe the mushrooms and cut in half, or slice if large, and add to the bowl with the olives.

Place all the ingredients for the dressing in a bowl, and whisk until smooth.

Line the salad bowl with the rinsed salad leaves, then place the salad ingredients in the center. Sprinkle with the rock salt and chopped parsley and serve with salad dressing.

Serves **4 to 6**
Preparation time **5 to 8 minutes**

2 cups canned artichoke hearts, drained
    and sliced
1 cup cherry tomatoes
1 cup baby button mushrooms
$\frac{1}{2}$ cup pitted black olives
$1\frac{1}{2}$ cups assorted salad leaves
Rock salt
2 Tbsp chopped fresh flat-leaf parsley

DRESSING
$\frac{2}{3}$ cup sour cream
1 to 2 tsp Dijon mustard
2 Tbsp olive oil
1 onion, chopped fine
2 Tbsp capers
1 tsp superfine sugar

ZESTY ORANGE COLESLAW

IF YOU HAVE A FOOD PROCESSOR WITH A SHREDDER OR GRATING ATTACHMENT, USE IT TO SHRED THE CABBAGE. IT SPEEDS UP THE MAKING OF THE COLESLAW CONSIDERABLY.

Serves **6 to 8**
Preparation time **12 minutes**

3 cups finely shredded fresh white inner cabbage leaves
2 large carrots
2 large oranges
1 orange bell pepper, seeded and chopped
4 oz yellow cherry tomatoes
½ cup golden raisins
2 Tbsp chopped fresh flat-leaf parsley

DRESSING
6 Tbsp olive oil
2 Tbsp orange juice
1 Tbsp grated orange zest
1 tsp prepared mustard
Salt and freshly ground black pepper

Place the cabbage in a bowl.

Peel and grate the carrot, peel and divide the oranges into segments, then cut the segments into small pieces. Add the carrot, orange bell pepper, tomatoes, and golden raisins to the cabbage. Toss lightly.

Place all the ingredients for the dressing in a screw-top jar and shake vigorously. Pour over the cabbage mixture, toss lightly, then turn into a salad bowl. Sprinkle with the chopped flat-leaf parsley, and serve.

TOSSED GREEN SALAD

CHEESE-BASED FONDUES ARE FILLING, SO A GREEN SALAD AND SOME CRUSTY BREAD ARE OFTEN THE ONLY ACCOMPANIMENTS NEEDED.

Serves **4**
Preparation time **10 to 12 minutes**

1 garlic clove, halved
1 Romaine lettuce
½ small cucumber
3 celery stalks, trimmed and chopped
1 green bell pepper, seeded
2 chicory heads
6 scallions, trimmed
1 large, ripe avocado
2 Tbsp lemon juice
2 Tbsp roughly chopped parsley

DRESSING
5 Tbsp olive oil
2 Tbsp white wine vinegar
1 tsp Dijon mustard
Salt and freshly ground black pepper
1 to 2 tsp superfine sugar

Rub the garlic inside the salad bowl. Rinse the lettuce leaves, pat dry, tear into small pieces, and place in the bowl.

Peel and dice the cucumber. Add to the lettuce with the celery.

Slice the pepper into half-moon shapes, and add to the bowl. Pull the chicory heads apart, rinse, then arrange in the bowl.

Chop the scallions and scatter over the lettuce. Peel the avocado and discard the pit, dice, toss in the lemon juice, then arrange in the salad bowl with the parsley.

Place all the dressing ingredients in a screw-top jar. Shake vigorously until well blended. Pour over the salad, toss, and serve.

ARTICHOKE HEART SALAD

A VARIATION ON THE EVER-POPULAR WALDORF SALAD, THIS SALAD IS SURE TO BECOME A FAVORITE WITH YOUR FRIENDS AND FAMILY, AS IT HAS WITH MINE. IF YOU PREFER, THE ARTICHOKE HEARTS CAN BE REPLACED WITH CANNED WHITE ASPARAGUS OR PALM HEARTS.

Drain the artichoke hearts and chop into bite-size pieces. Rinse the lettuce, drain well, and arrange in a salad bowl.

Core and slice the apples and toss in 2 tablespoons of the lemon juice, then mix with the artichoke hearts, chopped celery, pecans, and grapes.

Blend the mayonnaise with the remaining lemon juice and the lemon zest, then add to the artichoke heart mixture and mix lightly.

Pile the mixture in the center of the lettuce leaves, garnish with celery leaves, and serve.

Serves **4 to 6**
Preparation time **10 minutes**

2 cups canned artichoke hearts
1 Romaine lettuce, roughly shredded
2 green dessert apples
4 Tbsp lemon juice
4 celery stalks, chopped
1 cup pecans
1 cup white seedless grapes
6 Tbsp mayonnaise
1 Tbsp grated lemon zest

TO GARNISH
Chopped celery leaves.

SPICY PEPPER & MUSHROOM SALAD

THIS COLORFUL AND APPEALING SALAD IS IDEAL TO SERVE WITH MANY OF THE FONDUES: TRY IT WITH THE BEEF, POULTRY, OR FISH RECIPES.

Serves **4**
Preparation time
   15 minutes
Cooking time **10 minutes**

1 red bell pepper
1 green bell pepper
1 yellow bell pepper
1½ cups button mushrooms
8 scallions, trimmed
   and chopped
3 Tbsp roughly chopped
   pitted black olives
Salad leaves

DRESSING
½ tsp crushed dried chiles
1 garlic clove, crushed
Salt and freshly ground black
   pepper
4 Tbsp olive oil
1 to 2 tsp liquid honey
1 Tbsp balsamic vinegar

TO SERVE
Freshly grated Parmesan
   cheese and basil sprigs.

Cut the peppers into quarters and remove the seeds and membrane. Line the broiler rack with aluminum foil, arrange the peppers on the foil, and place under a preheated broiler for 10 minutes or until the skins have charred. Remove the peppers, place in a plastic bag, and leave for about 10 minutes or until cool enough to handle. Skin and slice thinly, and place in a bowl.

Wipe and thinly slice the mushrooms, and add to the peppers with the scallions and olives.

Place all the ingredients for the dressing in a screw-top jar and shake vigorously until blended. Pour over the peppers and mushrooms and toss lightly.

Arrange the salad leaves on a serving plate and top with the pepper and mushroom mixture. Sprinkle with the Parmesan cheese and basil sprigs to serve.

CREAMY POTATO & APPLE
SALAD

THIS SALAD IS DELICIOUS SERVED WARM OR COLD.

Serves **4**
Preparation time
   10 minutes
Cooking time
   15 minutes

1 lb new potatoes
1 medium onion, chopped
6 scallions, trimmed and chopped
4 celery stalks, trimmed and chopped
2 dessert apples
2 Tbsp lemon juice
½ cup pecans
4 to 6 Tbsp mayonnaise
2 Tbsp plain or Greek yogurt
Salt and freshly ground black pepper
Lettuce leaves
2 Tbsp chopped fresh mint

Scrub the potatoes, cut in half, and cook in lightly salted boiling water for 15 minutes or until tender. Drain and, when cool, dice.

Place the potatoes in a bowl and add the chopped onion, scallions, and celery.

Peel the apples if preferred, then core and dice them, and toss in the lemon juice. Stir into the potato mixture with the pecans.

Blend the mayonnaise with the yogurt and seasoning, add to the potato mixture, and stir until lightly coated. Turn into a lettuce-lined salad bowl, sprinkle with the mint, and serve.

MINT & LEMON TABBOULEH

THIS DELICIOUS SALAD COULD BE SERVED AS AN APPETIZER AS WELL AS AN ACCOMPANYING SALAD.

Serves **6 to 8**
Preparation time
12 minutes plus 10 minutes standing time

- 2 cups bulgur wheat
- 4 medium tomatoes
- ½ small cucumber, peeled and diced
- 8 scallions, trimmed and chopped
- ½ cup raisins
- 2 Tbsp chopped fresh parsley
- 2 Tbsp chopped fresh mint
- 2 Tbsp grated lemon zest
- 2 Tbsp lemon juice
- 4 Tbsp olive oil
- Salt and freshly ground black pepper

Cover the bulgur wheat with tepid water and leave for about 10 minutes, stirring occasionally. Line a colander with a clean dish towel and drain the bulgur wheat, pressing out as much water as possible. Stir with a fork to separate the grains and place in a bowl.

Cut the tomatoes into quarters, and seed if preferred. Chop fine. Add the tomatoes and cucumber to the bulgur wheat.

Stir in the scallions, raisins, chopped herbs, and lemon zest, and mix lightly.

Blend the lemon juice and olive oil, season, then pour over the salad. Mix lightly before serving.

RED BEAN & PEPPERONI SALAD

THIS SALAD IS ALMOST A MEAL IN ITSELF. IF YOU ARE CATERING FOR BOTH VEGETARIANS AND MEAT-EATERS, SERVE THE PEPPERONI SEPARATELY.

Serves **4**
Preparation time
8 to 10 minutes

- 2 cups canned red kidney beans
- 3 shallots, sliced fine
- 1 red serrano chile, seeded and chopped
- 1 cup cherry tomatoes, halved
- 6 scallions, trimmed and chopped
- 2 cups sliced then diced pepperoni
- 1 Tbsp chopped fresh parsley
- 1 Tbsp freshly snipped chives
- 1 to 2 tsp Worcestershire sauce
- 3 Tbsp olive oil
- 1 Tbsp red wine vinegar
- Salt and freshly ground black pepper

Drain the kidney beans and rinse under cold water, before placing in a bowl with the shallots and chile. Add the tomatoes, scallions, pepperoni, and chopped herbs.

Blend the Worcestershire sauce with the oil and vinegar, and season to taste. Pour over the salad and toss lightly. Place in a serving bowl and serve.

DESSERTS

WHITE CHOCOLATE & TOFFEE SWIRL FONDUE

WHEN BUYING CHOCOLATE FOR COOKING, LOOK FOR THE BEST AVAILABLE. THE HIGHER THE COCOA BUTTER CONTENT, THE BETTER THE FLAVOR.

Break the chocolate into small pieces and place in the fondue pot with the heavy cream.

Place over a moderate heat and cook gently, stirring frequently until the chocolate has melted and is smooth and creamy. Carefully transfer to the lit burner.

Place the sugar, corn syrup, and butter in a small pan and heat gently until blended. Remove from the heat and stir in the light cream.

Carefully pour the toffee sauce on top of the white chocolate fondue in a swirl, then serve with the fresh fruit and cookies for dipping.

Serves **6 to 8**
Preparation time **5 minutes**
Cooking time **6 to 8 minutes**

8 oz white chocolate
$2/3$ cup heavy cream
2 Tbsp raw brown sugar
1 Tbsp corn syrup
2 Tbsp butter
2 Tbsp light cream

TO SERVE
Pear and pineapple wedges, strawberries, hazelnut sponge and Italian biscotti cookies for dipping.

LUSCIOUS VELVETY CHOCOLATE
FONDUE

THIS FONDUE IS DEFINITELY NOT FOR THE FAINT-HEARTED. IT'S RICH AND DECADENT—
ABSOLUTELY HEAVEN ON EARTH. AS WITH ALL DESSERT FONDUES, THIS CAN BE PREPARED
IN THE POT AND SERVED WITHOUT PLACING OVER A LIT BURNER: THIS WILL MAKE THE
FONDUE EVEN MORE LUSCIOUS AND WICKED, AS IT THICKENS UP ON COOLING, GIVING YOU
MORE CHOCOLATE WITH EACH DIP.

Break the chocolate into small pieces, place in the fondue pot, and
pour in the cream, rum or Cointreau, and sugar if using.

Place over a moderate heat and cook, stirring frequently until melted
and thoroughly blended.

Carefully transfer the fondue pot to the lit burner and serve with the
amaretti, chocolate chip cookies, strawberries, and banana pieces,
speared onto the fondue forks as dippers.

Serves **6 to 8**
Preparation time **5 minutes**
Cooking time **6 minutes**

8 oz semisweet baking chocolate
1 cup heavy cream
3 to 4 Tbsp rum or Cointreau
1 Tbsp granulated brown sugar,
 optional

TO SERVE
Amaretti cookies, chocolate chip
 cookies, strawberries, and
 banana pieces for dipping.

NUTTY MILK CHOCOLATE FONDUE

WHEN YOU ARE GOING TO SERVE A DESSERT FONDUE IT IS ESSENTIAL TO PLAN ANY APPETIZERS AND THE ENTRÉE CAREFULLY. THE DESSERT WILL BE VERY RICH, SO SERVE LIGHTER COURSES BEFOREHAND.

Serves **4**
Preparation time **4 to 5 minutes**
Cooking time **6 to 8 minutes**

8 oz milk chocolate
1 to 2 Tbsp maple syrup
$^2/_3$ cup heavy cream
2 Tbsp rum
$^3/_4$ cup roughly chopped
   toasted hazelnuts

TO SERVE
Apple wedges and orange segments (allow one whole fruit per person), tiny meringues, and pirouette cookies for dipping.

Break the chocolate into small pieces and place in the fondue pot with the maple syrup, cream, and rum.

Heat gently, stirring frequently until the chocolate has melted and is smooth and creamy.

Stir in the hazelnuts and serve with the pieces of fruit, meringues, and pirouette cookies for dipping.

MAPLE & CINNAMON FONDUE

BOTH FRIENDS AND FAMILY WILL BE BOWLED OVER BY THIS DECADENT AND DELICIOUS FONDUE. IT IS SO GOOD YOU WILL BE LICKING YOUR LIPS FOR HOURS!

Serves **4**
Preparation time **3 to 4 minutes**
Cooking time **5 minutes**

$^1/_2$ stick butter
$^2/_3$ cup granulated brown sugar
$1^1/_2$ tsp ground cinnamon
$1^1/_2$ cups light cream
2 Tbsp maple syrup
2 Tbsp cornstarch

TO SERVE
Strawberries, melon balls, pineapple and mango wedges, ladyfingers, and graham crackers for dipping.

Place the butter with the sugar and a teaspoon of the ground cinnamon in a saucepan, and heat gently until the sugar has dissolved. Stir well. Bring to a boil and cook for 1 minute.

Stir the cream and syrup into the pan. Blend the cornstarch with the tablespoon of water and stir into the pan. Cook, stirring until the mixture thickens.

Pour into the fondue pot and carefully place over the lit burner. (If the fondue is overheated it will burn slightly—if this starts to happen, remove from the heat for a short time.) Sprinkle with the remaining cinnamon. Serve with the fruit and cookies for dipping.

BRANDIED ORANGE
FONDUE

FOR THIS FONDUE IT IS WORTH USING FRESHLY SQUEEZED ORANGE JUICE RATHER THAN FROZEN CONCENTRATE. IT IMPROVES THE FLAVOR AND YOU HAVE THE ADDED BONUS OF ATTRACTIVE FLECKS OF ORANGE IN THE FINISHED FONDUE.

Serves **4**
Preparation time **3 minutes**
Cooking time **6 to 8 minutes**

8 oz semisweet baking chocolate
$\frac{1}{3}$ cup freshly squeezed orange juice
4 Tbsp heavy cream
2 Tbsp brandy
1 tsp grated orange zest

TO SERVE
Profiteroles, ginger cookies, chocolate mints, and marshmallows for dipping.

Break the chocolate into small pieces and place in the fondue pan with the orange juice. Heat slowly until the chocolate has melted, then stir until smooth.

Stir in the cream and heat gently. Stir the brandy into the fondue with the grated orange zest. Heat, stirring, until the mixture is smooth and creamy.

Place over the lit burner and serve with profiteroles, ginger cookies, chocolate mints, and marshmallows for dipping.

BLACK CURRANT CREAM
FONDUE

IF YOU USE SWEETENED BLACK CURRANT JUICE, OMIT THE SUGAR FROM THE RECIPE. HOWEVER, IF USING FRESH BLACK CURRANTS, POACH THEM GENTLY WITH WATER AND SUGAR TO TASTE, THEN BLEND IN A FOOD PROCESSOR TO FORM A SMOOTH PURÉE.

Serves **4**
Preparation time **3 to 4 minutes**
Cooking time **5 to 7 minutes**

2 cups black currant juice or purée
1 to 2 Tbsp lemon juice
2 to 3 Tbsp superfine sugar, or to taste
1 cup heavy cream
2 Tbsp port or Madeira
1½ Tbsp cornstarch

TO SERVE
Banana pieces, strawberries, seedless grapes, pineapple wedges, macaroons, and baby meringues for dipping.

Pour all but 2 tablespoons of the black currant juice or purée into the fondue pot and stir in the lemon juice, and sugar to taste.

Place over a very low heat and heat gently until warm. Stir in the cream, and port or Madeira.

Blend the cornstarch with the reserved black currant juice or purée, then stir into the fondue pot. Cook, stirring until the juice thickens. Carefully place over the lit burner.

Serve with the fruit, macaroons, and meringues for dipping.

CREAMY MALLOW FONDUE

FOR THIS FONDUE I HAVE USED MIXED SUMMER BERRIES, BUT IT WORKS EQUALLY WELL WITH JUST RASPBERRIES OR A MIXTURE OF STRAWBERRIES AND RASPBERRIES. AS WITH ALL SWEET FONDUES, DUE TO THEIR HIGH SUGAR CONTENT, THERE IS A TENDENCY FOR THE FONDUE TO BURN SLIGHTLY. IF THIS HAPPENS REMOVE FROM THE HEAT AND ALLOW TO COOL; YOU CAN STILL DIP THE FRUITS AND COOKIES IN.

In a food processor blend the berries to a purée, then pour into the fondue pot. Add the marshmallows and cream.

Place over a very low heat and cook gently, stirring frequently until smooth. Take care that the mixture does not boil. Stir in the lemon juice, then carefully transfer to the lit burner and serve with the marshmallows, ladyfingers, macaroons, and apple wedges for dipping. If the fondue starts to burn slightly, remove from the burner for a while, but continue to dip.

Serves **4**
Preparation time **3 to 4 minutes**
Cooking time **10 minutes**

8 oz mixed summer berries,
  thawed if frozen
2 cups marshmallows
⅔ cup heavy cream
1 to 2 Tbsp lemon juice

TO SERVE
Marshmallows, ladyfingers,
  macaroons, and apple wedges
  for dipping.

DARK CHERRY FONDUE

BUY CANNED PITTED CHERRIES AS THIS WILL SAVE A LOT OF TIME. IF YOU WISH TO USE FRESH CHERRIES YOU WILL NEED TO POACH THEM GENTLY IN A SUGAR SYRUP FOR 10 TO 15 MINUTES FIRST.

Roughly chop the cherries. Stir 1 cup of the cherry juice into the cream. Pour into the fondue pot, stir in the sugar, and place over a gentle heat. Bring to a gentle boil, then stir in the cherries and kirsch.

Blend the arrowroot with 1 tablespoon of either cherry juice or water, then stir into the fondue pot and cook, stirring until the fondue thickens.

Carefully place over the lit burner and serve with the meringue fingers, marshmallows, fruit, coconut, and shortbread fingers for dipping.

Serves **4**
Preparation time **5 to 8 minutes**
Cooking time **8 minutes**

2 cups canned pitted black cherries, reserving the juice
2/3 cup heavy cream
1 Tbsp superfine sugar
1 Tbsp kirsch
1 Tbsp arrowroot

TO SERVE
Meringue fingers, marshmallows, pineapple wedges, melon balls, cubes of fresh coconut, and shortbread fingers for dipping.

INDEX